DOES EDUCATION HAVE A FUTURE?

PLAN EUROPE 2000

PUBLISHED UNDER THE AUSPICES OF THE

EUROPEAN CULTURAL FOUNDATION

PROJECT 1
EDUCATING MAN FOR THE
21st CENTURY

Volume 10

DOES EDUCATION HAVE A FUTURE?

The political economy of social and educational inequalities in European society

---

DOES EDUCATION HAVE A FUTURE?

THE POLITICAL ECONOMY OF SOCIAL AND EDUCATIONAL INEQUALITIES IN EUROPEAN SOCIETY

by

JARL BENGTSSON, Sweden
ALBERT VAN DEN BERG, The Netherlands
ALAIN GRAS, France
BARRY HAKE, United Kingdom, Co-ordinator
IGNACE HECQUET, Belgium
IAN LISTER, United Kingdom
JÜRGEN ZIMMER, West Germany

with the collaboration of

DIETER BERSTECHER, West Germany
GASTONE TASSINARI, Italy

MARTINUS NIJHOFF / THE HAGUE / 1975

This study has been realized with support of the Shell Group of Companies and the European Cultural Foundation.

ISBN-13: 978-90-247-1760-6 e-ISBN-13: 978-94-010-1693-3
DOI: 10.1007/978-94-010-1693-3

TABLE OF CONTENTS

PREFACE

This volume has been prepared in the framework of Project 1: "Educating Man for the 21st Century" of Plan Europe 2000, sponsored by the European Cultural Foundation. While most of the studies launched under this Project deal with specific aspects or levels of education the present volume attempts to provide a more global view of educational futures and their relationships to alternative futures of the overall socio-economic system. It should not be considered as a general integration or synthesis* of the different studies of the Education Project of the European Cultural Foundation – although it draws on them as well as other recently published documents. Rather, it should be regarded as one of several possible approaches, analytical tools, and incentives to the study and open discussion of educational problems seen in a long-term perspective.

The volume is the result of a collective effort of a multinational team of researchers. A colloquium of some sixty participants, meeting at the University of York in October 1972, provided critiques and comments to the first version of the report. But only the authors themselves claim responsibility for the methodology of the study, and the opinions and conclusions expressed therein. These do not necessarily reflect those of the sponsors of the volume, the European Cultural Foundation and the Scientific Committee of its Education Project.

* Such a synthesis will appear as the concluding report of the Project.

CHAPTER 1

APPROACHES TO THE PRACTICE AND PLANNING OF SOCIAL AND EDUCATIONAL CHANGE

It may be assumed that certain social and educational trends will continue to develop in the short term. Those seeking change will have to accept them as given constraints to be overcome in the success of their own strategies. Who makes the real decisions to support or oppose certain developments is, however, not clear. The choice of futures will not be the decision of any one social agency or social group. It will be decided by a multiplicity of decisions taken by different groups in a variety of social situations with varying degrees of power and influence to implement their aspirations. These choices and decisions are, and will continue to be, often capricious or purely opportunist. In many cases decisions actually influencing the future will not be recognized as such by those responsible for them or by those subject to them. The future is very often either an unconscious dimension of everyday existence in the street as in the classroom (Galtung 1970a).

What purpose can the presentation of possible alternatives for the future of education and society serve in the present situation? What do they say about how things change in moving towards one or other possibility? The simple answer is that we do not know which trends will dominate and which will remain of little influence in the future. This will be determined by action on the part of people. To suggest a number of possible long-term solutions to present problems is only the first step in working for the future. The next step is to choose between those possible solutions as objectives, and to develop the action most appropriate to moving in the right direction. For the student, parent, teacher, politician or administrator engaged in the everyday reality of education and its constraints, the question is very mundane and yet vitally important – "What do I do on Monday morning?" Given this context of educational reality, the purpose of possible social and educational futures is to stimulate awareness of basic options. They can be used to analyze and identify dominant tendencies and potential alternatives in the present situation. The long-term implications of ongoing practices and innovations can be understood in a broader context. Possible futures can be used to distinguish between and classify various proposed innovations in official reports and the actual implementation of policies in legislation. This can be done in the case of reports such as the Joxe committee on the reform of secondary education in France (1972), the White Paper of the British Minister of Education (1972), the policy statement of the Dutch Minister of Education (*Beleidsnota* 1972), legislation in Sweden and France introducing permanent education and the proposals of the German Federal and *Länder* Ministeries in relation to the reform of higher education. These reports and various forms of legislation make statements about the goals of education, the structural forms, the curriculum and teaching methods and the allocation of resources. The same applies to proposals by interest groups in education such as teachers organizations, student bodies, associations of parents, and various activist groups. Comparing their diverse proposals against possible futures of different kinds can enable us to examine and think through the present educational system and ideas for its reform. Using possible futures also has the advantage of suggesting a broader range of possible solutions to the problems concerning various groups. This may suggest other courses of action, the need to modify present concerns, and to reconsider priorities in the allocation of resources. Consideration of possible alternative solutions to present problems can inform and illuminate attempts to deal with those problems in the present. The purpose of long-term studies of the future of any social activity is to awaken people to their own responsibility for determining what the future could and should be, and not to tell them what it will be. We justify long-term thinking about the future in terms of the increasing importance of long-term planning in the European countries. This is largely based on extrapolative forecasting and trend-planning techniques which do little more than justify the series of short-term decisions taken by dominant groups in the existing social order. Long-term planning based on trends is unlikely to do more than perpetuate the present.

There are no trends of the future except those of the past and present which some social groups wish to maintain in the future. The two main dangers to be avoided are presenting the future as a copy of the present, and being utopian in an a-political sense. Only within a comprehensive long-term framework can decisions be subjected to an adequate analysis of their social motivation and consequences. In thinking about the future of a sector of social activity such as education, any forecasts made have to take into account more widespread changes in the social system and in social conditions. Traditional forecasting techniques do not easily lend themselves to this type of futures-thinking because they tend to neglect the interdependencies between education and the wider society. We cannot talk about the future of education if we restrict our frame of reference to the traditions and conventions governing the closed world of education which are reflected in quantitative trends in expenditures, enrolments, qualified outputs etc. If we accept as a basic premise that education and society are inseparably linked in social reality it is vitally necessary that a first step in prospective thinking about education should be a coherent analysis of social and educational dynamics. It should be no surprise, therefore, that controversies surrounding various approaches to social forecasting are reflected here. Our ideas will be, indeed already have been, seriously challenged and criticized because we emphatically dismiss extrapolative techniques of forecasting as the legitimate form of futures-thinking in long-term planning. We regard this approach as leading neither to an adequate analysis nor understanding of the social forces shaping the future of European society and education. Dominant forms of long-term planning at the national and European level do little to contribute to the pressing need to work and plan towards a desirable future for Europe.

The approach adopted here is the tentative exploration of the social and political factors likely to be operational in the next thirty years, and of their potential consequences for education. We do not hope to persuade those readers who are either cynical of any attempt to think meaningfully in the long term or those who are doubtful of the "scientific" respectability of our particular approach. However, we can present some idea of the way we intend to develop it here. Consequently, this introduction begins by critically examining some of the dominant approaches to thinking about the future. This is followed by some considerations of a new role for the social sciences in relation to social development in what we regard as a "constructive approach" to social and educational planning. The recurrent theme, in this introduction and the report as a whole, concentrates on the role of the social sciences in explaining social and educational inequalities and their potential contribution to planning in response to these inequalities.

A CRITICAL ANALYSIS OF APPROACHES TO FUTURES-THINKING

1. Surprise-Free Approach

The standard approach to studying the future is the extrapolation of present trends into the future. This is to envisage the continuation of dominant forms of social development without considering possible obstacles and assuming no basic discontinuities. Such an approach contributes to "surprise-free futures" (Hake 1973a). The major assumption is that the main factor in social change is the impact of scientific knowledge and technological innovation upon society. There is a belief that social conflicts concerning the nature of society and its future development have been surpassed by the "end of ideology" (Bell 1967). Conflicts are interpreted as disagreements about the distribution of material resources available in society. The standard works on futures reflect these main centres of interest – Kahn and Wiener (1967), Fourastié (1966), Bell (1967), Richta (1968). "Post-industrial" society is the single future towards which all mankind is moving. Consequently, the post-industrial society sounds surprisingly like the industrial society of today, the only difference being that it will be a society characterized by a rapid rate of change in its quantitative dimensions. This extrapolative view of the future leads to a view of the future as an extension of the present. Economic goals and technological development assume a basic importance to this continued growth model of the future, and the "Western growth ideology" is held out to the Third World as the only possible future open to them. This growth ideology argues that there will be an increasing convergence of different societies under the influence of technological change with similar economic, political, family and educational structures.

The dominant form of futurology suffers from the traditional teleological weaknesses of social theory. It can be considered as an addition to dominant theories of social development. The social theory of the nineteenth century, propounded by Comte, Durkheim, Saint-Simon and Spencer, postulated a theory of "industrial society" towards which all societies converged through a series of developmental stages of social evolution. The destiny of all societies was to follow the path shown by the industrial nations of Western Europe and to incorporate the necessary institutions and values dictated by the evolutionary ladder. The future is already colonized (Freire 1970).

Strategies for using technology in the service of dominant values and goals assume a great significance. The tendency towards technological forecasting, and an increasing concentration upon social technologies, are central to the control dimension of such a society. Behaviour expectations are expressed as capacities in individuals and groups for adaptation to changes in their physical and social environment. In the extreme case this approach demands that we change our values when these stand in the way of the requirements of technological development. The application of advanced planning techniques appropriate to this viewpoint in the major decision-making agencies suggests that somebody has an interest in this type of future, whether its goals are legitimate to all or not (Jantsch 1969).

The possibility of discontinuity, hence possible social disruption and alternative uses of technologies, are easily overcome in the standard view of the surprise-free future. It assumes the capacity of society to eradicate its remaining marginal problems of poverty, deprivation and disadvantage through the assumed "spin-off" of continued economic growth. The role of this optimistic future in drawing attention away from the acute social differences and the powerlessness of specific social groups in the present is clearly indicated by the popularity of its thesis to dominant groups in capitalist, social democratic and socialist regimes in advanced industrial societies. While silent in terms of immediate conflicts, problems and issues of the present, they are now concerned with the future of industrial society – the post-industrial society. The new "science" of futurology has a strong base in the West among the think-tanks and research institutes, such as the Rand Corporation, and the Hudson Institute of the Future, and most European countries have at least one such institute involved in futures research of this nature. The social bases of these activities are indicated by the financial support of international organizations, national governments, industry and private foundations. The situation is little different in the socialist countries of Eastern Europe, where resources are increasingly being pumped into futures research, albeit of a "non-bourgeois" form (Kahn 1972).

The similarities between the visions of the future are not all that different between the West and East, perhaps thus supporting the hypothesis of "post-industrial society" as a convergence of capitalist and socialist societies. The surprise-free future denies the contingency of the existing social order in human society, and projects an image of the future which consolidates the status quo and the present distribution of social power. It provides the techniques and skills of an advanced look-out function for dominant groups, warning them of impending crises to be avoided if they are to maintain their power over the future. Potential crises have to be avoided if the future is to be insured as "surprise-free".

2. The Crisis Approach

The self-fulfilling prophecy of the surprise-free future has come under increasing attack predominantly from the viewpoint of the damage caused by the continuation of present growth rates (Peccei 1969). Problems of poverty, hunger, overpopulation and under-development have become more acute in the newly recognized "Third World" as the development gap widens. The triumphs of economic growth and technological development in advanced industrial societies are being increasingly questioned in terms of environmental pollution, ecological imbalance, potential exhaustion of natural resources, and population pressure. It seems that industrial society has given rise to new problems of an acute form. This may place its survival at risk and gives rise to the idea of crisis futures (Hake 1973a). The short-term perspective, the latent-ideology and the remarkable complacency of the growth thesis have been exposed by Ehrlich (1970), Mishan (1967), the Blueprint for Survival Group (the Ecologist 1972), and more recently, the Club of Rome report (Meadows 1972). The diagnosed crisis in the future points out the threats, to existing values and goals, of present strategies in economic and science policy (Gabor 1972). They pose the threat to the quality of life as a major factor in the demand to change these strategies. They do not specify what the precise content of the "quality of life" is for most people, let alone for different social groups. This hides the real problems by encouraging everyone to feel suddenly guilty and responsible for the multiple crises of industrial society. The natural greed and irresponsibility of individual men is put forward as the cause of the crisis rather than the contradictions of the social and political system. Simulation of the future in world models incorporating a limited number of non-social variables tends to act as a magic wand capable of reducing the social complexity of present and future reality. The chance of future catastrophy does not lead to a fundamental analysis of the social and political origins of the crisis. The world models are a-political and a-social in matters which are basically political and social. Which social groups will introduce the world manipulation which is required? The only practical political solutions are either a long-term process of re-education, persuasion and indoctrination, or the authoritarian imposition of restrictions upon individual freedoms. An outside chance might be a cultural revolution through a mass movement manifesting a radical change of values. However, this is only likely to occur when the crisis of economic development is too far advanced to enable adequate preventive and recuperative measures to be introduced.

The Club of Rome report, and its strategies of dynamic equilibrium, typifies crisis futurology because it fails to identify the political dimensions of the problem. It proposes a panacea for the removal of symptoms without identifying the real problems. While the surprise-free future suggests that basic inequalities will be removed by continued economic growth, the crisis future of the Meadows report touches only marginally on the problem of inequalities within the world system and they do not feature in the world model. World-wide crisis management can only produce a few superficial corrections and amelioration of conditions within the present distributions of social and political power. This is more likely to maintain the dependency of the Third World than lead to equal opportunities. In the advanced countries it is only too likely that limited growth will freeze existing inequalities than lead to redistribution. The redistribution of material goods and services is a function of the distribution of power in society and the political naïvety of "The Limits to Growth" and its irrelevance to the problems of under-privileged and disadvantaged groups in present and future society can only serve the survival of the existing system.

3. The Critical Approach

The surprise-free and crisis futures are distinguished from those critical of the existing and potential social system. The essence of the critical approach to the future is conflict rather than a consensus concerning the social values likely to determine the future (van Steenbergen 1971). Critical futurology assumes a basic value change to be occurring in present society and relates alternative futures to the values and goals of different social groups (Hake 1973a). The values of dominant social groups in the present, and those of potential dominant social groups in the future are the source of alternative goals for future society. Socially disadvantaged and radical minority groups in the present are seen as capable of bringing about radical change in the future. It is suggested that some social discontinuity or disruption is the result of a major redistribution of power in society. The location of alternative views of society in social groups indicates the distribution of social power and influence as the key to the future. Dominant values and goals in the present are manifested by élite social groups using technology to maintain the status quo into the future, while potentially new values and goals are manifested by radical minority groups in the present which seek to bring about change. To the degree that such a change needs to be preceeded by a major redistribution of power in society, the value change involved suggests some major discontinuity or disruption in society.

On the basis of radical groups of the youth culture Roszak (1969) has attempted to establish a counter-culture representing a new culture, while McHale (1971) has argued for certain vanguard groups as indicating a new value system arising from the values of identified minority and radical social groups. Reich (1971) has envisaged a new consciousness as leading to the "greening of America". While the critical approach is characterized by the consideration of alternative value systems, it is also characterized by a lack of concern for the strategies essential to the implementation of the alternatives suggested. Consequently, suggested futures tend to resemble the classical utopias in vaguely prophesying some future era of bliss. They propose some image of the future based on general and vague assumptions about human nature, needs and capacities. The indication of value alternatives lacks coherent statements as to the source of the social discontinuity and the nature of the social dynamics essential to their implementation. Their self-determining man, who will be free in the future, is being subjected to real factors of change in the present. Consequently, the concentration upon some proposed change in values and social discontinuity can promote deterministic views of the future on behalf of underprivileged and powerless social groups. The future can be distorted into an idealistic utopianism lacking any reference to the possibility of the proposed futures being realized through appropriate strategies of action in the present. Like the surprise-free and crisis approach, the future proposed by critical thinking can take on the characteristics of sophisticated "cargo cults", promising the millenium at the ideological level, but without a realistic assessment of the probabilities of their realization.

Critical thinking about the future may perform a counter-ideological function equivalent to seeing the future as a continuation of the present. New currents of social ideas and practice do not represent a new society, but rather a new image of society (Willener 1971). Idealistic utopian thinking, divorced from the social action of social groups, is as dependent on the intervention of some promised external or non-social influence as the technological determinism of the surprise-free future. Critical approaches may concentrate upon alternative images of the future on behalf of underprivileged and powerless groups, but without any reference to the possibilities of their coming about. They distort the real aspirations of underprivileged and powerless groups in whose interests they are supposed to speak. They too often lack of constituency among these groups because of their inability to deal with concrete problems in the present.

TOWARDS A CONSTRUCTIVE APPROACH TO THE FUTURE

The surprise-free, crisis and critical approaches are inadequate to thinking constructively about the future. They support attempts to take the problem of the future out of public debate, to depoliticize what is a question of choice. The great danger of the various forms of futurology is that their authors are among the social groups who are predicted to become the most influential and powerful in the future society. Not for the first time in human history is the legitimating ideology of a "new society" produced by the group whose interests that ideology will serve.

These various futures add additional stages of development to the linear conception of social evolution – from industrial society to some form of post-industrial society. The old story receives various new final chapters but the basic plot remains the same – attention is drawn from present difficulties and anxieties and a new confidence is given in the future. The hero remains the same – science and technology remain active in the transitional present as the main determinants of the future – whether their influence is optimistically or pessimistically interpreted. However, the detective seems to be missing from the story. There is little attention to any clues indicative of potential changes in values and problems of social conflict and power in shaping the future are almost ignored. It is the problem of power and vested interests in present society and between different kinds of society that the futurologists conveniently escape. The story also lacks a clear role for the actors engaged in the plot. Little scope is given to the possibility that conscious social action could change the development of technology in pursuit of different value systems (Hampden-Turner 1971).

If futures research has given little attention to why certain futures are envisaged, even less attention has been given to the interests of the people whose future is being investigated. Futures research serving the interests of people and meeting the needs of their present situation has been a matter of little concern. There are a number of opposing models of future society. The solution of the conflict between these alternative futures probably arises from the purposive action of social groups with particular complexes of beliefs, values and interests. Conflicts between these views may give rise to divergent rather than convergent social tendencies. Analysis of the future of society should take into account conflicts and potential discontinuity in future developments, and indicate their possible social roots and location in the present. The only constructive way to overcome the sterility of most thinking about the future is to see society as a struggle between different views on the realization of the full potential of men. This requires the social scientist to no longer concern himself with the future as a problem of social order, i.e. how society operates as a self-regulating and self-maintaining system, but to turn to problems of social power, i.e. how men can gain control over essentially man-made institutions and social development in the future.

Plausible answers to the future development of society have to be sought within the concrete reality of the present and the relationships of social groups. A true understanding of the processes of social change cannot be achieved by an assumption of the harmony of interests between and within societies. Such an assumption serves to divert attention from the basic forces shaping the future of society. In rejecting conflict as a source of change it is a useful instrument in defending and rationalizing the interests of dominant groups and meets their need to overlook the realities of inequality and exploitation in the present. Rejection of the harmony of interest may stimulate a dichotomisizing view of society but it also recognizes differences of interest between groups in society. It is a rejection of the dominant view that the development of science and technology are autonomous processes to which man and society have to adapt. The development of science and technology in society cannot be separated from other social processes such as the formation of interests and conflicts between interests within and between societies. Present directions in the development of science and technology are neither autonomous nor inevitable, and certainly not independent of the play of social forces (Kuhn 1962).

Science and technology, interpreted as man-made possibilities, can serve the interests and goals of diverse social groups. This can mean the use of such possibilities either for the domination or the emancipation of men. Any future society which develops in Europe will use science and technology to achieve the ends of social groups seeking to maintain or change the existing situation. The constructive style of futures-thinking suggests that the alternative images of the future held by these groups should form the basis for consideration of future strategies. The problem of choice raises the question of the values and groups with which we align ourselves in working for the future. This may have major implications for the nature and degree of participation in the long-term planning process, but above all for the role of the social scientist in that process. The development of a constructive style of futurology leads to a concern with the possibilities for social change. This involves the process of developing the instrumental means necessary to realization of desired goals. These possible futures may be seen as futures which clearly and explicitly state the different values and goals systems possible in the future, locate these in specific social groups, and indicate the strategies and means appropriate to their realization.

This introduces the action component into our concern with the planning of the future. Constructive social action oriented towards the future is derived from knowledge of contradictions in social reality. It takes form in pragmatic attempts to resolve these contradictions in concrete situations. We cannot know the future, but we can identify possibilities and the means of their attainment. Action to produce one or other of these possibilities through the goal-oriented action of individuals and social groups is based on appropriate technical capacities. In studying the future the social sciences can play a role in facilitating the critical awareness of social groups about their collective and individual rights. They can enable these groups to actively participate in developing the strategies appropriate to the future development of society in their interests (Horowitz 1967). The service function of social science justifies social research which serves more or less directly the interests of those who are usually the objects of research. The often praised "relevance" of social research can be interpreted as providing a fundamental analysis of the existing social order taking into account the various sources and forms of conflict. In particular, relevant research should focus on the interests of different groups composing society in terms of the contradictions between dominant social values and actual social conditions (Gramsci 1959). Social research activity should become an integral element of social change which is characterized by an experimental approach towards planning and policy formation.

This is not a case of "us" going out to help "them" in the traditional form of "do-gooders", but giving such groups the knowledge and skills to deal with issues which really matter to them. The issues taken up may be extremely instrumental, e.g. housing, unemployment, urban resettlement, health, transportation, educational facilities, but will be linked to fundamental analysis of the social structures which give rise to "their" problems. To claim the right to live on its own terms is the social right of every social group to "say their own word" (Freire 1970). Enabling people to become conscious and involved in matters regarding their own interests, and to choose between alternative courses of action, is distinctive of constructive futurology. It is also the fundamental distinction between those who emphasize the use of social research within the existing social order, and those who view it as an instrument of social change. The social sciences can show how man is living in a world which is not biologically or technologically "given" but which has been constituted in an historical process of social action, and possesses a future which will be also so created. They can argue the contingency of the social order as a social construction, and oppose the legitimation of the social world as a natural order. Society can be organized in different ways and the social sciences have the potential to demystify the existing social order through their reflection upon the links between social conditions and the interests of social groups. The social sciences can develop critical evaluations of the social order which may support a different *Lebenswelt* – a different distribution of power and wealth, and new patterns of social relationships. This suggests at least the potentiality of a different social order and the possibility of conceiving alternative futures which differ from the present. To what extent there are chances of possible alternatives being realized depends on the knowledge of the power relationships in the existing society.

Future oriented social research can explain social relationships in concrete terms and indicate alternative possibilites. In doing this it can act as a critical guide to policy-making. If the right of people, ordinary people, to free self-development is recognized and supported in practice, there is some hope of furthering the process of social emancipation (Wertheim 1973). This may be a utopian view, but the existence of a utopia as a utopia per se is a necessary condition for its potential realization (Kolakowsky 1971). The realization of utopian vision is only possible when it is supported in social practice. Social inventions and new forms of living in society remain utopian within the present circumstances of social influence and domination. A utopia is simply the mirror-image of the constraints encountered in present society. Social science can be of service in this process to the degree that it can serve both the interests of control and emancipation, it can function against and on behalf of groups of people. The practice of reflection and criticism on the part of social scientists is the only way in which the development of scientific activity can produce social research which responds to the needs of people. Social science is an essential instrument of social planning and policy without which the emergence of a "qualitatively different" society cannot be expected. The future can be seen as a challenge to man's creativity rather than as a repetition of the past (Freire 1970).

Since surprise-free and crisis styles of futurology are unable to reflect upon dominant social interests, and critical futurology is not able to relate to the technical possibilites for the realization of its projected images of the future, they are equally unable to contribute to the analysis of the contradictions of present society. Constructive futurology, linking goals and technical possibilities in social action can enable us to break through these ideological functions and see the future as open rather than closed. To the degree that the future is perceived as open and problematic, it becomes a political issue.

CONCLUSION

The "constructive" futures-thinking used here is characterized by the attempt to relate a number of relevant and important factors of social and educational systems, and to question how these are developing towards the future. The most important factors in social and educational systems are those concerned with the equal and unequal distribution of social power and rewards. These characteristics of social life are at the basis of many conflicts and tensions in society. The future represents possible solutions to contradictions in present society. Thinking about possible futures for society and education entails making statements about future possibilities of the resolution of basic problems in the present. The tentative presentation of alternative possibilities and future dynamics relates certain states that are possible in the future to the present structure of social and educational developments. They can be used to bring out the basic contingent nature of existing society and confront it with alternatives. We suggest some of these conflicts between societies, within advanced industrial societies, and in education as our basic point of departure in Chapter 2.

Using this approach we construct four alternative futures representing different solutions to these conflicts. We must emphasize that these social alternatives are only four of an infinite number which may be imagined, but are the logical results of the variables used in our analysis. The alternative futures presented in Chapter 3 may look better or worse than the present. This will be influenced by the ethical, psychological and social characteristics of the observer and his normative evaluation of his social situation. We go no further than suggesting these models of the future as images of the future of society which may provide a possible framework for analyzing certain problems and their possible solutions in the future. In the sense that they suggest either the maintenance or change of prevailing social conditions they may serve to clarify certain aspects of present reality. They do not "unveil" the future in any sense, but may facilitate a better understanding of the consequences of present decisions about the future of society.

As a matter of empirical and logical fact we do not, and cannot, know which aspects considered typical of the present structure of education will prevail in the future. The most we attempt in Chapter 4 is a statement of four possible models, which are to be seen as representing alternatives and not historical stages of development. We discuss some issues concerning the tensions and dynamics within and between the models, although we do not attempt to suggest the chances of realization of any one model. We do stress that all four alternatives discussed are possible in relation to the present structure of European educational systems, and are based on historically established patterns of thought and action. We purposefully leave the question of future dynamics and transition to the reader and his capacity to relate the models to his understanding of social reality and social situations as developmental possibilities. Some guidelines for the analysis of concrete situations are given in Chapter 5. These examples seek to illustrate the future as a consequence of decisions taken today and tomorrow.

CHAPTER 2

TRENDS AND PROBLEMS IN SOCIAL AND EDUCATIONAL EQUALITY

The commitment of politicians in all countries to the virtues of industrial society, and their optimism in the emerging post-industrial society, simplifies problems of social and educational equality. Their main internal problems are seen as the application of the increasing wealth produced by their rapid economic growth to irradicating the few remaining areas of poverty and material deprivation (Lipset 1964). Equality of social opportunity is seen as provided by the redistribution of the economic surplus produced by their own growth and the application of the newly discovered tool of social progress-technology. In their external relations there remains great optimism in the capacity of the industrialized countries to assist the underdeveloped countries to achieve modernization. Economic growth and technological development are seen as gradually making the world into a replica of western industrial society. The Western model of industrialization, urbanization and affluence is still seen as "the whole world's future happening now".

However, industrial society has not delivered the goods expected of it. During the nineteen-sixties it became clear that the consensus about the values and goals of modern society had broken down in a very profound way. The very society which epitomized the model of industrial society was torn apart by internal racial strife, the revolt of its own youth, and became deeply involved in a major neo-colonial war in a developing nation. The mid-sixties witnessed the revolt of youth in the European countries on an extensive scale, which almost toppled an elected government in May 1968. These problems cannot be considered as discrete and isolated local difficulties for which clear solutions are readily available. Attempts to do so can be no more than treatment for the symptoms of deeper contradictions in present European and world society, and suggest a form of crisis management in modern industrial society. Industrialization is a Pandora's box, posing a *problematique* of interrelated questions and difficulties in development.

The problems of present social organization are closely related to the development of rationality and the application of scientific principles and technological development to social development (Habermas 1971). The dominant ideology inhibits any consideration that increasing rationality in social organization might have negative social effects. Yet the very societies which are the most ardent supporters of such rationality have experienced a variety of anti-social and irrational forms of extremism. Characteristically, these movements have been interpreted as temporary breakdowns in the general trend towards increased rationalization in social relations. The revolt against rationality, and more specifically the identification of technology as the scapegoat for our social ills, is closely related to the kind of society and principles of social organization so seriously pursued in industrial society.

While science and technology have increased the potential of social and individual development, the prevailing opportunities to take advantage of these possibilities is very unevenly divided within and between present societies. Scientific and technological development have contributed to new forms of inequality while removing earlier patterns of social differences. Indeed, the present direction of their development has added to existing inequalities through their tendency to support monopolization of power and resources in society (Baran 1970). The uneven division of scientific and technological capacities is a persistent contradiction in industrial society, however much they may profess an ideology of the equality of all men as rational beings. The interdependence of advantage and disadvantage is a cumulative result of their basic rationalization tendencies (Frank 1967). The advantage of the few explained as the disadvantage of the many is to be found in domestic and international inequality in control over power and resources in modern society, and more specifically in questions concerning the role of education in the distribution of life chances.

PROBLEMS IN THE INTERNATIONAL SYSTEM

The recent enlargement of the European Economic Community is a phenomenon of great significance, not only for the internal changes which it will bring about within Western Europe itself, but also for its role in the balance of world power. The external relationships of the EEC to other major industrial societies will be largely determined by the same forces which have given rise to the internal shape of Europe as an international system in itself.

The present movement of European integration is largely characterized by the aggregation of nation states into a comprehensive economic system as opposed to a social system. As these nations become more interdependent in economic terms, however, they continue to maintain distinct political systems and cultural differences. While economic activity is increasingly rationalized in the form of the multi-national corporations, often extending far beyond Europe, there is no equivalent political superstructure. This leads to a fundamental asymmetry in the growing international specialization and division of labour and the political capacity to control that development at the European level. Furthermore, attempts to overcome the segmentation of political institutions have been limited beyond government institutions. The organization of trade unions on an international level has not given rise to an effective counterweight to the multi-national corporations, thus allowing them to increase their capacities to manipulate political systems. There is a tendency at the European level to restrict participation in decision-making, to reduce the number of issues declared to be political, and to increase the area where administrative and technical criteria apply. The overall result is a depoliticizing of issues and problems at the European level and their removal from adequate public control. This reinforces the continued support of private control of economic activity by governments as a reaction to competitive pressures. The expansion of a large market and the concentration of control in large corporations at the European level leads to European integration on the basis of economic and technological rationalization.

It is in relationship with the Third World that the economic and political basis of the enlarged Community become most clear and disturbing. A specific reflection of the high rates of economic growth in Western Europe has been the great increase in the migration of workers from the semi-developed countries surrounding the geographical boundaries of the Community and from Third World countries. Such migration has become a major source of semi- and unskilled labour for the growth economies of the advanced industrial nations. This has the potential of forming a new sub-proletariat in the advanced countries characterized by their inferior working and living conditions and subjected to more general social discrimination (Visalberghi 1973). The problem of this migration has only very recently become a "hot issue" in the industrialized countries. It is an area for short-term crisis-management by national governments in response to specific domestic problems arising from this trend. National governments neglect the long-term dimensions of the problem and treat isolated aspects of the issue in national terms. How far does migration of labour increase the dependency of the semi-developed countries and the monopoly power of the advanced countries? This question points out the high priority needed to be given to the migrant labour problem at the European level, and not purely in terms of the domestic economic and social interests of the advanced countries.

The more general relationship of the enlarged European Economic Community to the Third World is of increasing importance. There is a tendency for this to be left to national governments and the multi-national corporations, and no common aid policy is yet discernable. This situation has a number of consequences which probably do more to protect the interests of the advanced industrial countries than to promote those of the underdeveloped countries of South America, Africa and Asia (Hayter 1971). Policies based on the dominant theory of development have produced a widening gap between the rich and the poor nations in the interests of the already developed countries. The problem of capital investment in the Third World has been largely resolved by the extensive activities of multinational corporations on the one hand, and the provision of financial loans, both interest free and interest bearing, on the other hand. In the former case the investment of capital retains the centre of control in the advanced countries and results in the repatriation of profits to the shareholders in these countries rather than their reinvestment in the developing countries (Jalée 1968). The present structure of development aid in providing markets for the industrial countries is now being extended in the search for and control of strategic materials supplied by the poor countries. The search for strategic resources adds to and increases the control of the poor by the rich through the process of development. Capital has facilitated the incorporation of the Third World into world trade on terms which perpetuate their dependence and the persistance of the inequalities of the market system (Mason 1970).

The dependence of the Third World nations is also perpetuated by the inability of the industrialized countries to allow the free transfer of technological knowledge and capacities. The transfer of technology occurs largely through the investment of the multinational corporations, thus maintaining the monopoly power of these corporations. Moreover, these may be quite the wrong technologies in terms of the Third World. The bulk of technological research and development in the advanced industrial countries is geared to the capital-intensive and skill-intensive technology appropriate to high income products. Technological transfer too often involves the transfer of inappropriate technologies and products which serve a minority of the population in the developing nations in consumption terms and does not serve the majority in terms of employment. There is increasing evidence of the "marginalization" of a significant proportion of the labour force in the Third World as a result of technological transfer in terms of their being not only unemployed but also unemployable. Development policy has produced this result through its tendency to support a small élite rather than the technologically and economically backward majorities (Mandel 1970). Industrialization has indeed been initiated with a certain measure of success, but this has tended to reinforce inequality in the developing nations and produce a greater dependence on the advanced industrial countries. This is very obvious even in the case of agricultural development. Rather than supporting the growth of the domestic market, agricultural development – the Green Revolution – has emphasized large-scale agricultural technology to produce crops for the mass markets of the advanced countries. The commitment to the international market for primary products, as opposed to the domestic market, is perpetuated by the need to earn foreign currency to pay for the modern equipment, fertilizers and pesticides imported from the developed countries. The concentration upon the transfer of inappropriate technologies has tended not to create expected new employment opportunities but has turned under-employment into simple unemployment. The transfer of modern technology and its sophisticated products to the Third World has created new forms of inequality within those countries and between advanced and developing countries (Kidson 1970).

The question to be answered is whether the poor societies are poor because they are poor, or are they poor because the control and appropriation of resources by the rich make them poor. Does this impede the development of their real and potential resources and the capacity of their populations to be productive and creative?

CLASS AND EQUALITY IN EUROPEAN SOCIETY

The advanced industrial countries of Western Europe retain various forms of social inequality. Inequalities persist in the allocation of rewards, the distribution of resources and in patterns of social recruitment. More specifically there remain differences in educational opportunity, occupational chances, income from employment and property, and housing and leisure facilities. These inequalities can be observed in the everyday life of modern society, together with tensions arising from the unequal distribution of rewards. These are structured inequalities generated by a market-based system of distribution supported by the political system in providing a number of safety valves reducing pressure for change. The relative inaction of underprivileged groups in the face of their inequality is probably explicable in terms of the capacity of the market system of distribution to successfully veil the structured nature of their inequality (Parkin 1971).

The basis of the reward system in Western capitalist societies is the occupational order. The division of labour produces a hierarchy of broad occupational categories which represent different positions in the distribution of material and non-material benefits. However, it is obvious that patterns of inequality are not determined by the economic system in isolation. Given the close links between dominant economic interests and political influences in industrial society, the role of the market as a primary source of inequality is supported by political and institutional arrangements which protect and legitimate inequalities. Among élite social groups there is a general consensus as to the justice and desirability of the institutional supports to inequality. It is suggested that the inherent needs or demands of the modern economic and technological order call for a specific form of distribution of rewards. Above all, the structure of differential rewards is important in producing the appropriate motivations and achievement aspirations necessary to recruit people to different occupations most efficiently. Consequently, the educational system, the legal system and social policies are instrumental in supporting that social order.

Furthermore, the stratification system comprises mechanisms which stabilize the system of inequalities. Whatever the ideological nature of society, there are opportunities for significant numbers of the lower socio-economic groups to achieve more advantageous positions in society through social mobility. While most social mobility is of a relatively limited nature, from one occupational group to a slightly more rewarding group, it does represent a personal solution to inequality. The hope of self-advancement thus serves to release some of the tensions arising from inequality and aspirations for social improvement support the reward structure.

There are important problems facing any society which seeks to increase the aspirations and stresses achievement values through its educational system.

The increased competitiveness of capitalist society is more likely to produce casualties among the lower classes, who do not possess the social and cultural attributes necessary to success, but are subject to the achievement ethic. Values of achievement may tend to maximize the development of available talents at the cost of serious frustrations among the "failures". Acute tensions are most likely to arise among those who experience low status especially at the point of access to the labour market. Attempts to overcome this experience are all too likely to entail symbolic attacks upon the social system. It is almost inevitable that the capitalist system of market competition should give rise to increasing degrees of juvenile delinquency, crime, rejection of authority and unrest among those groups who most severely experience the strains of low status. It is significant that such phenomena present no fundamental challenge to the structure of rewards and rules of distribution in society. The acting out of discontent in symbolic forms becomes irrational in that it effects no influence upon the social conditions producing the inequality (Goldthorpe *et al.* 1968).

Industrial society encourages accommodation to the facts of inequality; rather than presenting a challenge to inequality it encourages the incorporation of the unequal in the very system producing their inequality.

Social inequality in the distribution of life chances in modern European society does not go unchallenged. Left-wing political movements have based their ideologies, to a greater or lesser degree, on radical change in the rules governing the distribution of rewards and have based their political support on members of the underprivileged social groups. The egalitarian critique of the reward system has objected to the disparities in advantage for different occupational groups. Its interpretation of the reward structure is in basic opposition to that prevailing in Western Europe. However, this egalitarian view of inequality is challenged by the meritocratic critique of distribution according to the market system. The meritocratic principle is less concerned with the existence of unequal rewards to different occupational positions and more concerned with the inefficient market system which permits social rather than pure ability to predominate.

There appears to have been a gradual movement of socialist parties from the egalitarian viewpoint towards a form of socialist meritocracy in the Western European countries. In other words, the socialist movement in Western Europe has been gradually "deradicalized". Earlier radical ideas for the redistribution of social rewards have been eroded. This has occurred during the three decades following 1945, in which almost every European country has experienced at least one period of government by socialist or other left-wing parties. The key issue in this period has been whether the various forms of "social democratic" parties can manipulate the reward system successfully when the means of production are still held in private hands to a large degree. Educational reform has been seen by social democrats as an important means of redistributing life chances, and the educational reform debate is engaged in a political debate about social advantage and not a discussion of education *per se*.

The one measure of difference to stand out between countries with a greater experience of socialist government and their neighbours, is that they display a relative openness of the hierarchy of rewards as manifested in their educational systems and mobility rates. There can be little doubt that social democrats have been more willing to accept a broadening in the social basis of recruitment to privileged positions rather than to promote the equalization of rewards to different social positions. Consequently, there has been a tendency among socialist parties, and the social democratic countries, to support a meritocratic interpretation of socialism by putting competition on a more socially equitable basis. While this meritocratic view of socialism is obviously at odds with the traditional market system and supports greater political intervention, it differs basically from the egalitarian viewpoint (Crosland 1956). These two positions are basically incompatible in the understanding of classlessness. Meritocratic socialism supports a view of the classless society as being achieved by equal competition between social classes for advantage positions in the occupational structure and a breakdown of inter-generation inheritance of these positions. The view of egalitarian socialism, however, is that the distribution of unequal rewards should be abolished and classlessness be achieved through criteria of social need. The meritocratic view is compatible with the modern capitalist order of individual competition, while the egalitarian view fundamentally challenges that system. Furthermore, it should now be clear that the "equality of opportunity" vision of socialism dominates over the egalitarian view and is easily accommodated within the existing social order. Historically, it would appear that this trend, away from egalitarian to meritocratic socialism, has occurred during the period of increasing affluence in the European countries and continues unabated. It can be argued that the general improvement in the material conditions of life has reinforced the meritocratic socialist view that increased economic growth can in itself produce greater prosperity. It is ironic that socialist governments are probably the most committed to economic growth with little concern for the actual proportion achieved by the less advantaged from that increased social product. Increased productivity, often by the disadvantaged, is seen as a more important factor than the redistribution of rewards from the advantaged to the less advantaged (Crosland 1971).

On the basis of such an understanding it is necessary to ask very basic questions concerning the influence of the European Community upon equality. Does it manifest trends towards the market system, the meritocratic or the egalitarian principle of social distribution of life chances? We become sceptical when we consider the European level redistribution of opportunity between the urban/industrial and the rural/agricultural regions. Furthermore, given the balance of ideological influence in the enlarged Community, especially the resistance of the social democratic countries to become involved, we question the possibility of a radical critique of the operational principles of the Economic Community. The prospects are not encouraging. A critique of the Community's systems of distributing rewards requires a macro-social interpretation of the reward system and an understanding of the systematic nature of inequality. Such a critique is far removed from accommodation to the system, and the incorporation of the labour movement and the social democratic parties in the amelioration of the patterns of access to unequal social positions. The prospects for a radical critique of the organization of the Community structure are far from optimistic. It is all too likely that the need to gain higher standards of material well-being, as a result of economic growth, will predominate over problems of redistribution. The most likely result will be a tendency for accommodation in the form of the instrumental collectivism by trade unions for a greater share of the social surplus. This may produce limited material gains for the less advantaged but will certainly not challenge the basic patterns of inequality in modern European society. Given the concentration of the social democratic party of the most significant recent entrant into the Community upon the price of butter, it is most probable that a deradicalization of the European working class will dominate European politics in the short term.

PROBLEMS OF EDUCATIONAL AND SOCIAL EQUALITY

Recent developments in the European countries have made clear the centrality of education in the promotion of social equality. Educational practices with origins in early industrial society have been increasingly interpreted as barriers to social and individual progress in the advanced industrial societies of Europe. Reform of school and university structures and the modification of curricula at all levels have been stimulated by changes in the broader social context of education.

Since 1945 the most important single objective of educational policies has been that of expansion – expansion which serves a number of purposes and with a number of important consequences. In the first place, expansion has served to promote the extension of "educational opportunity for all" and the equalization of educational opportunity. This has resulted from the general consensus that educational opportunity is an essential right of the individual in modern society. Secondly, a major objective in educational policy has been the increasingly felt need to make the educational system more relevant to changing economic needs. There is an increasing trend for educational systems to become more involved in the adequate supply of trained manpower for economic activity. Old skills become redundant, and new skills are developed calling for increased education and training.

Thirdly, there has been a growing awareness that the growth of scientific knowledge and technological advancement have radically influenced the knowledge and skill requirements of most jobs and professions. Education must prepare a greater percentage of the population to deal with this fundamental change (Cros 1969).

While there are as yet no organs for planning educational development coherently at the European level, there is a remarkable resemblance in the main characteristics of the educational strategies evolving in the different European countries. There has been a remarkable growth in the international market for the export and import of educational ideas. The international agencies, such as UNESCO, the Council of Europe, and the Centre for Educational Research and Innovation of OECD, have also played their part in the exchange, and increasing similarity, of educational ideas and practices in different countries. The main developments in policies in both Western and Eastern European countries follow identifiable key trends despite apparent differences in their overt political and educational ideologies (Poignant 1973).

In the first place, changes in the structure of education are leading to the gradual, universal development of the comprehensive or common secondary school, the extension of the compulsory period of schooling until 16 or 17 years, and moves towards the integration of academic and professional branches of higher education. The need to provide greater equality of opportunity has led, secondly, to the introduction of discrimination, in favour of disadvantaged social groups, in the form of compensatory education at the pre-school level. Thirdly, major changes are occuring in the curriculum available particularly at the primary and secondary levels of school. In general, this takes the form of a reduced significance for early choice between academic and vocational choice, and the extended relevance of general education in secondary education especially. We find an increasing emphasis, fourthly, on the application of new educational technologies to the individualization of learning systems (Hake 1973b). Finally, the recent recognition that learning is a never-ending process, has recently given rise to the idea variously known as permanent education, life-long learning, continuing or recurrent education. These ideas collectively form the orthodoxy of educational policies in most European countries and provide the basic framework for thinking about the future of education (Janne 1972).

These developments are clearly manifested in projections for further educational growth in the future and maintain the expansionist image into the seventies and eighties. The German *Bildungsrat* envisages 50% of young people achieving the *Abitur* by 1980, compared to a level of 9.9% in 1968 (*Bildungsrat* 1969), while the French *Commissariat du Plan* has forecast that the full-time enrolment of 18 year-olds will reach 100% by 1985. Such future perspectives are mainly based on an acceptance of the achievements of the countries with the highest enrolments in full-time education at present – the USA, the USSR, Japan and Sweden. To base one's view of future educational provision on the present standards of the most advanced nations tends to a view that the educational structures of the future are already germinating in current experiments and innovations, and that the development of the educational system cannot go beyond the generalization of the situations which are today regarded as the most advanced (Poignant 1973). Some sources regard the trends in the structure of educational systems as valid predictors for the future (Sauvy & Girard 1973). The following major forecasts for the future have been put forward:

1. an extension of pre-school education;
2. a quasi-generalization of secondary education;
3. a large extension of post-compulsory education (Poignant 1973).

However, present trends in official educational policy indicate that the commitment to expanding mass education is accompanied increasingly by efforts to restructure the organization of learning. Recent experience suggests that the substantial achievement of structural reforms will give way to greater concern for reform of the curriculum and introduction of new technologies. These changes, with increasing support from official agencies, are a further manifestation of the need for schools better equipped to meet the general developments in society. There can be little doubt that educational decision-makers will pay more attention to rational curriculum development and learning systems. Cost-consciousness by educational authorities encourages the search for new methods reducing per capita expenditures. There is a growing consensus that these developments will characterize the forward-looking schools of the future. In terms of increasing enrolments at all levels, the extension of compulsory schooling, the development of comprehensive schools, innovations in curriculum and educational technology, as well as more effective strategies of compensation and orientation, the dominant and powerful image of the future is one closely identified with the continued development and consolidation of the patterns of achievement of the recent past.

The essential question is whether these trends promise a radical change in educational provision. They are often claimed as an educational "revolution" (Richmond 1970). Does the dominant image of the future of education promise a major qualitative change in education or is it an extrapolation of the quantitative expansion of the present system? Do the policies presently being followed provide the necessary answers to the profound questions of mass education in advanced industrial society? Or are they forms of liberal idealism which maintain the basic structure of education, and by extending the provision of education seek to keep hopes of success alive? Although much has been reformed and is being made more efficient, there has been little radical change to merit the description of an educational revolution in the long term. It can be said that such policies are bound to leave the crucial social and educational issues unanswered and to continuously face crises to which there are no simple solutions and certainly no panaceas.

Contemporary educational decision-making may be characterized as a classic case of crisis management responding to a series of external pressures of an economic and political nature. As each new crisis is faced, the system is maintained by making minor modifications, and each reform itself becomes the potential source of another crisis. This series of modifications becomes characterized as "the educational revolution", and an image of the system as flexible and dynamic is articulated. The social basis of this dominant ideology of educational development becomes clear, however, when we begin to ask questions such as who is learning? What is being learned? How is it being learned? and Where is it learned? and Who is providing the answers to these questions and in whose interests.

A brief analysis of some key issues illustrates the basic political dimensions of education development, and suggests that, if there is a crisis, it is in fact a social crisis concerning the distribution of power and resources (Drouard 1972).

The Equality Myth – Educational or Social Change?

The achievement of greater social equality through reform and expansion of educational provision is a frequently heard slogan in most advanced industrial societies. It is believed that more equal educational opportunity will provide that social equality. However, the experience of the last twenty years of rapid educational expansion has clearly indicated the limitations of education as a vehicle of social equality. The many changes in the scale and structure of educational systems have had little or no effect on the social disparities in educational participation. The vast increase in enrolments at all levels of education have left unaffected or even strenghtened fundamental social and educational inequalities (Huberman 1970). The OECD conference on Policies for Educational Growth in 1970 concluded that

a. there remained considerable social selection in education;
b. social disparities in participation persisted;
c. lower socio-economic groups manifested low achievements quite unrelated to measured ability, and

d. social differentials in the length of education were relatively unchanged (OECD 1971).

Social differences in schooling seem to manifest themselves at the beginning of school attendance and to widen through the experience of formal education. It appears that educational systems reflect society rather than change it, and that social inequalities become pervasive characteristics of educational processes (Bordieu & Passeron 1970).

It is clear that education seeks to expand social opportunities. It is also equally clear that it is far from being universally effective. Manipulation of educational variables in order to change levels of achievement does not deliver the expected returns. The measurement of educational achievement in practice stands for longer-term social changes supposedly produced by educational success, such as better occupational opportunities, higher incomes, levels of consumption, and use of leisure. Greater equality of educational achievement is not in itself the ultimate objective. Such objectives are essentially political in that they involve attempts to redistribute more fairly the social privileges bestowed by education. Evaluation of the broad range of social goals in equal educational opportunity policies is nothing less than the measurement of social and political change.

Nevertheless, we continue to evaluate broad programmes of educational and social reform in terms of purely educational criteria of measured achievement within the framework of the established school system. Such evaluation criteria do not challenge the predetermined power and social relationships which equality strategies are supposed to change. The problem of achieving greater social equality through education becomes more clear when we recognize the limitations of changing school variables to that end. The very limited success of equality of opportunity policies in the last twenty years means that future policies may have to look to the change of non-school variables in the wider society as of greater priority. If schools do no more than perpetuate and legitimize social inequalities, it may be necessary to change society first, and certainly to be less confident of the capacities of schools to promote social change. It is no longer possible to hide the fact that some social groups are chronically disadvantaged by the wider society and that education perpetuates that inequality. It may be that present educational practices, based on educational solutions to social problems, do more to preserve inequality in the wider society than to remove it. Social and educational policy makers should be either demonstrating clearly the effectiveness of school variables in achieving greater equality in the substantive redistribution of the life chances of all social groups, or earnestly looking for other ways of achieving this. Conventional wisdom and the monopoly of educational systems do not hold out much hope of bringing about real changes in social inequalities in the near future (Jencks 1971).

The Limitations of Schooling – The Hidden Curriculum?

The all too apparent limitations of schools in promoting greater equality is closely related to the fact that modern society and its educational systems are highly selective of those abilities which they take seriously and seek to promote. The question is one of which abilities, and which social groups and individuals, are assessed as possessing those abilities. This problem is further compounded by the relative closure of other means of demonstrating ability in modern society. Since the educational system is increasingly charged with the task of recognizing ability, it is very necessary to examine how formal schools perform this vital function in influencing the relative life chances of social groups and individuals. Are the achievements needed to demonstrate the possession of these abilities contributed by educational institutions or by factors outside the educational system itself?

It is now clear that certain children begin school at a disadvantage by virtue of a social milieu which is not conductive to educational success as defined in formal systems of education. Indeed, these disadvantages are more likely to be perpetuated and certified by the educational system. Consequently, large sections of the population are prevented by the social organization of education from demonstrating their ability to meet the criteria of educatability prevailing in educational systems. These factors have given rise to the idea of a "hidden curriculum" which is more powerful than the school itself. Our understanding of the "hidden curriculum" refers specifically to the influence of social background as a basic determinant of what is learned in schools, and therefore of educational achievement. This involves differences in attitudes and aspirations, and basic information about the educational system.

Apart from the extension of the period of compulsory education, equal opportunity strategies are largely based on social demand for education. The assumption of such policies is the provision of places in schools for all those who seek them and have demonstrated their ability to benefit from them. This means that those who have benefited most from recent expansion of education at all levels have been the children of middle class families whose family backgrounds support higher educational aspirations. There is ample empirical evidence of the operation of the hidden curriculum of non-school variables on social differentials in the distribution of educational achievement (Andersson 1970). Variations in social background are very closely related to the different reactions of middle and working class students to the demands of educational institutions. When considering the overall effectiveness of the school system in achieving its stated aims, the home, the peer group and the school are the important factors in order of priority. The longer-term influence of schooling on the distribution of life chances is even less than its influence on school based measures of achievement (Douglas 1969).

If the home is prepotent in relation to school performance, while peer group pressures are confirmed by school experience, these relationships support the widespread evidence of the continuity of social inequality between generations. The relative success of schools becomes a measure of confirming social differences (Bordieu & Passeron 1964). School achievement can then be interpreted in terms of the relationship between the role of school-based criteria of achievement in the recognition of ability, and the contribution of different social backgrounds to meeting established criteria of educatability. It is unlikely that greater equality will be achieved unless strategies are developed which influence either student's ability to meet these criteria or change the criteria themselves (Bernstein 1970). To the degree that public authorities can modify the school environment more than other factors, it is these factors which have been manipulated in school reforms to enable more students to meet the criteria of educatability.

However, the relative impotence of school variables suggests that differential achievement will be difficult to remove while the intellectual and social criteria of success are limited to specific social groups whose value-systems dominate the school system. It may well be that more radical pedagogic and non-pedagogic measures will be necessary if the built-in inequalities of the social demand approach is to be changed. The removal of material and financial barriers, as examples of attempts to manipulate social factors in educational equality, has failed to a significant degree, and still leaves the problem of manipulating more subtle social background factors. The main policy implication is an extensive effort to modify the influence of the family and neighbourhood, with all the dangers of social engineering that this may entail. Alternatively it may be possible to change highly restricted and socially selective criteria of educatability and achievement dominant in the existing school system, but this entails a radical qualitative change in educational values (Bernstein 1970).

Social and Educational Disadvantage – The Need for Compensation or Emancipation?

While well tried educational reforms have had little effect on the major inequalities in education and society, educational agencies have recently embarked on more selective measures of a pedagogic nature. The rapid growth of programmes of compensatory education at the pre-school level is essentially directed at the inequality of specific social groups in terms of their educatability and potential achievement. The recognition of the importance of early socialization in educational achievement is leading to an extension of efforts to influence educatability through the development of intervention strategies. Compensatory programmes mainly seek to improve the skills of literacy and numeracy basic to the linguistic and cognitive demands of the school system, and can be seen as attempts to simulate the socialization of middle-class children prior to the commencement of compulsory education (OECD 1972). The rapid extension of compensatory programmes in most European countries does little more than illustrate intervention strategies as attempts to give the child the necessary capacities to fit the school rather than changing the school to fit the child.

There are very powerful assumptions about educatability, learning and the idea of the "good pupil" behind these developments (Keddie 1971). The tendency of school to favour and give priority to middle-class skills and attitudes goes unexamined, and non-achievers are defined as educationally disadvantaged compared to school-based criteria of educatability. The home background and the child itself become the responsible factors and their deficiencies as "deficit systems" are stressed. Schools claim the credit for the success of the middle-class home background, while assuming no responsibility for the under-achievers from the working-class. There is no recognition of any possibility that the schools may contribute to educational failure nor of any need to change the structures of schools to make learning more successful for the disadvantaged. The extensive support for compensation overlooks the direct contribution of schools to educational deprivation through the consensus of interests stressing the superiority of the culture of the school and the resistance of lower-class children to educational influences.

The ideological nature and social bias of compensation are clarified when we consider the relatively limited results of intervention strategies in North America and Europe. In most cases any gains made during the compensatory pre-school programme have almost disappeared within twelve months of completing the programme and entering normal schools. Such experience suggests that the very slight long-term effects may arise more from the fundamental lack of change in the assumptions and values of formal education. The essential problem lies in later school experience rather than in the preschool years. This may indicate that greater concentration should be given to changing and improving later educational programmes. While students are increasingly required to invest heavily in education and schools gain increased power in society, we are less certain of the nature of the inequalities involved in definitions of disadvantage. If educational disadvantage reflects broader social disadvantage we cannot expect the school to compensate for society. Continuity in the unequal distribution of life chances and influence in society are difficult to eliminate through a process of schooling which confirms and reproduces them (Baudalet & Establet 1971).

The evaluation of reform policies seeking to promote social and educational equality is only slowly moving beyond allowing economic necessity, familial obligation and social inequality to take their logical effect within the framework of present social differences. The achievement of substantive equality in society may require new approaches involving more radical policies geared to the role of education in promoting social emancipation. If educational disadvantage is fully recognized as a reflection of social disadvantage, i.e. basic inequality of life chances, the essence of equality programmes may need to be directed by positive discrimination. This means discrimination between the educational needs of unequal groups in society and developing the strategies appropriate to achieving greater equality between them. A radical policy of education for social equality would not seek to compensate for social inequality, but would seek to develop strategies of emancipation enabling the less than equal to participate fully in society with the long-term aim of changing and removing the sources of social inequality (Bengtsson 1971). Can educational change change the balance of power within education and between social classes within society? Can it involve social groups in the redistribution of life chances and resources in society and ask basic questions about the legitimacy of educational provision?

The Comprehensive School – Meritocracy or Equality?

One of the basic components of educational policies intended to promote equality of opportunity is the comprehensive school. The reorganization of selective secondary education into the common secondary school is interpreted as a radical change in educational provision (OECD 1971). It is also possible to view the postponement of selection in the lower grades of the comprehensive school, through the development of orientation periods, as an attempt to reinforce the role of the school as a centre for the distribution of educational values and attitudes. There is a tendency to view the comprehensive secondary school as a panacea for the problems of equal opportunity when in practice the basic problem is one of the values and attitudes transmitted by these schools. Are comprehensive schools to be meritocratic institutions that extend the opportunities for increasing numbers of children to compete for places in higher education, or are they to be institutions offering the possibility for all pupils to develop their different abilities? There are numerous contradictions in policies of comprehensive schools seeking either an achievement-based meritocracy or a socially engineered equality (Marsden 1970).

Since they tend to incorporate the educational assumptions and practices of selection and discrimination, comprehensive schools may create an intensified and more effective barrier to the development of talents not identified by the criteria of academic achievement. The gradual differentiation involved in orientation procedures designed to meet individual differences may merely reinforce the hierarchy of recognized ability in formal education. To a large degree the various forms of internal organization of comprehensive schools, such as tracking, streaming, ability grouping, mix-ability groups and orientation classes, only serve to reproduce the same predictable differentials as selective schools (Ford 1970). While change at the organization level is a necessary precondition of common schooling, it is not sufficient for the abolition of social differentials in achievement. The equal representation of the social classes and ability group in socially engineered comprehensive schools fails to question what equality means in the everyday workings of these schools. The obvious trend in comprehensive reforms away from the earlier objective of promoting social equality towards the more efficient promotion and selection of ability suggests the failure of the supporters of comprehensive education to work out systematically the relationships between home background and educational achievement. Changes in the organization of secondary education are largely based on false premises, because they fail to see beyond improved access to formal education as solutions to social and educational inequality. Comprehensive education based on the manipulation of school based variables ignores the evidence that social inequality is caused by factors over which the school has little control (Benn & Simon 1970).

The overall result of comprehensive schools may be to postpone the social and educational selection inherent in the formal educational process while making such selection more efficient. There is a general trend at the secondary level of schooling for examinations to take on the form of preparatory selection. The growing emphasis on general education in place of vocational education in secondary schools supports the view that extended general education performs a purer form of selection than early differentiation. It is not without importance that the orientation classes, which are intended to allow individual differences and capacities to manifest themselves, are characterized by a general curriculum. The growth of general education in the comprehensive secondary school is a major factor in distinguishing between educational systems based on "sponsored" and "contest" systems of mobility. The comprehensive school movement gives an impression of radical change in educational provision, but in fact minimizes the problems of reducing social inequality through education. It supports the facile optimism of the dominant reform ideology. The essential problem of the comprehensive school is whether élites can be majorities.

Individualized Instruction – Controlled or Free Learning?

An important role is now given to educational technologies in the teaching process. The aim is to improve productivity and efficiency through the individualization of learning. The most widely accepted concept of individualization is the arrangement of learning processes in sequences which the individual student can follow at his own rate of progress. Individualized instruction takes numerous forms but most efforts are concentrated on the development of learning materials, programmed learning, systems-based instruction, computer-assisted instruction and more ambitious ideas based on advanced communications technology (Taylor 1971). There is every confidence on the part of educational authorities that technology will play an increasing role in education in the future. This even extends to a view that educational technology could mean an end to the traditional classroom and even the school. Its introduction is often posed as a radical change in education, taking instruction into a new era of systematic and controlled techniques (Ziegler 1972).

It is possible that in individualized learning the individual gains access to selected mental skills quite independent of the learner. Increasing rationality in the transmission of knowledge and skills may lead to an adaptive process of learning without concern for the interests and motivations of the learner. The rational organization of learning, by presenting units of instruction related to the level of achievement of the individual, and building on individual differences and abilities, may only reinforce the consensus assumptions about educational objectives. This view assumes that the ends of instruction are known, that they are prescribed for the learner, and that he is expected to reach them. There are more fundamental criteria to learning than the ability of learners to learn certain concepts and the possibility of arranging appropriate units of instruction. What can be measured behaviourally at the conclusion of a predetermined instructional unit is not necessarily meaningful learning. Traditional measures of achievement dominate the development of individualized instruction, and support the psychometric model of learning in which the individual is more or less successfully initiated into accepted forms of knowledge as a passive entity. The application of rationality to the planning of instruction is vital to an educational system which maintains an unequal distribution of knowledge and skills in society. It reduces the learner's influences upon what, when and how he gains knowledge and reinforces the control dimension of the hierarchical relationship of the learning experience.

Wider issues of authority in the learning process and the learner's control over his own learning are largely ignored. Despite the ideology of radical reform individualized instruction may mean learners have less control over their activities. The widespread faith of educational authorities in educational technologies in solving the dysfunctions of present school systems may have much to do with their concern for the "how?" rather than the "what?" questions. This faith does nothing to overcome the basic alienative tendencies in individualized instruction. The privatization of the learning experience in individualized instruction may contribute to an increase in control over the learning process, and paradoxically lead to competition between isolated learners. Above all, the tendency to individualization may work against the ability of students to work together and learn from each other (Suppes 1973). It is difficult to see how human and social knowledge and skills can be learned outside of the group situation unless individualization is a strategy of control aiming to reduce group consciousness and increase manipulation of the individual.

Given the weaknesses and inefficiency of the traditional education system, it is very tempting to turn to educational technology for salvation. Individualization of instruction does not mean any necessary radical change in the content or organization of learning. When introduced by dominant interest groups, they tend only to produce more of the same education with greater efficiency. The individualization of instruction may be interpreted as a manifestation of increasing capacities in modern society towards social engineering, while the nature of control in society is far from being changed by new technologies. In relation to the control of social and educational change it is possible to regard new educational technologies as a diversion or at the most essentially marginal to real change in education or society. Technological innovations, with considerable commercial interests involved, run counter to any real change in education and tend to divert attention from the more basic issues.

Education as an Economic Investment – A System of Surplus Production?

Common to the policies of rapid educational expansion is the idea that expenditure on education is an investment promising faster economic growth and social development. This idea is closely related to the theory of a causative link between the level of educational development and the economic maturity of society (Denison 1967). The manpower approach to educational planning is an outgrowth of this idea. The supporters of rapid expansion of education on economic grounds usually argue that:

1. a high level of education is necessary to meet the manpower needs of a highly developed economy,
2. education investment leads to a faster rate of economic growth through increasing personal incomes, and
3. that there is an increasing need for highly qualified scientific and technical manpower in modern society (Harbison & Myers 1964).

These arguments can be interpreted as a rationalization of the trend for educational systems to be more closely linked to the selection, recruitment and allocation of manpower in the interests of the production system's commitment to economic growth.

The relationship between educational and economic development is far more complex, and the continuing expansion of education on economic grounds is faced by numerous problems. Technological influences on the occupational structure are extremely difficult to forecast as a basis for educational planning and the relationship between the qualified outputs of education and occupational requirements is very uncertain. The insufficiency of our knowledge of the links between education and the economy is now apparent in current problems facing educational authorities. There is increasing evidence that the expansion of education has in many occupations exceeded the demand for labour. Furthermore, the shift in the real technical requirements of many occupations has been far less than the rise in certification requirements now demanded for those occupations (Folgar & Nam 1965). The unthinking expansion of education may achieve little more than the creation of surplus production which in the short-term can only result in the devaluation of the qualifications and diplomas provided by education (Passeron 1967). Consequently school and university graduates increasingly have to accept jobs with lower status and income than they could have expected in the past. The overexpansion of education can result in no more than a "great training robbery" in which there is a poor correlation between either educational qualifications and subsequent job performance, or education and job expectations (Berg 1970).

Surplus production by the educational system is, moreover, no new experience for the developing countries, where educational provision far out strips the job opportunities offered by their level of economic development. The introduction of systems of formal education in Third World countries have mainly produced unemployment at all levels of qualification from primary school to the university level. The tendency of formal education to recognise only limited marketable skills has tended to underestimate the variety of skills available in the developing countries and certainly those most appropriate to their economic needs (Coombs 1968). The panacea of formal education for economic development is reflected in both the presence of an educationally generated unemployment and a high level of illiteracy in the Third World. Systems of formal education in the developing countries are all to often drawn from foreign models of education which evade the real problems of the need for skills. The provision of an educational system appropriate to the Third World can probably only evolve to the degree that it rejects models of formal education imported from the advanced industrial countries. The financial burdens of a system of formal education and the relevance of educational provision could lead to the redirection of investment to more directly productive forms and the relation of education to preparation for working life in the form of meaningful activity in the local community. The emphasis on formal schooling may make it a barrier to the promotion of the skills of innovation most vital to the development of the Third World. It is not insignificant that the recent critique of formal education has its sources in the developing countries. It is ironic that the advanced industrial societies of the West will probably experience in the future the same phenomena of high levels of educationally generated unemployment.

While there may well exist some general relationship between levels of economic development and the educational system, it is much more likely that economic growth will determine the percentage of an age group which one can afford to keep in full-time education. Education is more probably a consumption good influenced by social demand – the wealthier economic growth makes us, the more education we can afford irrespective of its relevance to economic and technological needs. The higher the level of economic development, the more it may be necessary to keep a larger proportion of people in education because of the threat of unemployment. The expansion of education, rather than promoting economic growth, may serve to take up on slack in employment for young people and compulsory schooling take on the form of "the great lock-up" in which "those out of work are confined, and those confined are given work" to occupy their time (Foucault 1961). Whatever the economic returns of investment in education to the individual and the economy, the certification function of the school in selection for jobs makes it individual economic suicide to drop-out of extended formal education. Is the holding power of schools maintained through their monopoly of marketable qualifications in a situation of surplus production of those qualifications?

Permanent Education – Resocialization or Self-development?

In modern industrial society the problem of achieving equality of opportunity becomes more difficult to resolve as education must provide social and occupational opportunities for an increasing proportion of the population in a situation characterized by rapid change in the occupational structure as a result of technological development. The response of educational authorities has been to pursue the idea of permanent education throughout life, which has the primary aim, in most formulations, of enabling more people to adapt to the changing demands of the labour market for new skills and qualifications (Council of Europe 1971). Permanent education in this sense entails a more flexible system of vocational and professional education closely related to changes in the structure of occupational differentiation and manpower needs. The concept of "recyclage" of individual capacities and qualifications illustrates the close links between the idea of permanent education and the so-called manpower approach to educational planning. With its stress on adaptation to changing technological requirements in the production system, permanent education may represent an educational strategy seeking to integrate the individual more effectively in the formation of the labour force (Bengtsson 1971).

Despite the general acceptance of the idea of permanent education by public authorities there are strong possibilities that it could reinforce existing social and educational systems based on competitive and acquisitive economic motivations of individuals in present society. It is possible that a system of permanent education based on an extension of formal education into adult life could have the potential of increasing the impact of social variables in education rather than reducing their influence. From this viewpoint permanent education could be a further rationalization of the selective mechanisms of education but which produces a more efficient system of distributing life chances in society. Furthermore, the dominance of economic and technological factors in formulations of permanent education give rise to fears that it could become a nightmare of compulsory alienation and adjustment problems. It could be a system of adaptive "life adjustment" education throughout life or a process of resocialization for the needs of the production system of industrial society. This would be certainly the case if it is an addition to and extension of the school-based model of education. It is all too likely that the development of permanent education in the present structure of most European societies will be palliative, a further soporific instrument of social control simply adding to the concentration on certification functions in modern education. This is very likely to be accentuated in the case of key professions in the service industries of a growth economy (Frese 1972).

Moreover, the fact that the number of qualified people is beginning to outrun the number of available jobs means that a utilitarian approach to permanent education will be faced by increasing contradictions. Economic and technological changes in the labour force are increasingly marginal to the more important social and political problems facing individuals in modern society. Capacities for understanding and dealing with these problems call for adult education enabling people to participate fully in social processes and especially decision-making on a democratic basis. It could be that permanent education should be more concerned with challenging the close relations between education and the certification process and allow more people to participate in decision-making in work situations and society in general. This approach could support experiments in new forms of social change determined by people themselves in their own interests (Frese 1972). It could in particular concentrate on the needs and interests of those who fail in the formal school system rather than seeking to keep them within that system in the hope of success. Life-long learning should be the right of the individual and not a compulsory requirement imposed by an extended system of schooling. Are we in danger of turning society into a school?

General Education – Occupational Selection or Social Skills?

Changes in the curriculum of secondary schools have been occurring with increasing intensity in recent years in most European countries. This mainly entails the extension of general education in the curriculum, especially in those sectors which have traditionally been regarded as directly preparatory for employment. The development of the comprehensive school and the extension of compulsory education have hastened this trend. This modernization of the curriculum involves a modification of the humanistic and literary bias of the elitist general education of the past, and the introduction of more scientific, mathematical and technical contents. General education gains in importance while changing its nature in the process.

This overall trend to general education in the advanced industrial societies has a number of sources in broader social developments. The tremendous increase in the social stock of knowledge and skills, especially its scientific and technological components, have led to changes in the definition of the valued knowledge and skills which education should transmit. This has brought to the forefront of educational debate a challenge to the traditional content of general education and arguments for inclusion of more valid and relevant knowledge appropriate to an increasingly technological society. The greater importance of science and technology in general social and cultural development has largely supported an attack on the elitist forms of encyclopaedic general education in European schools. Arguments for the inclusion of new subjects to generate greater interest in science and technology are based on their increasing social importance in modern culture and the change in society's dominant values (OECD 1971d). This culture is more complex and the need to educate a larger proportion of the population in newer forms of knowledge and skills gains in importance. Educational authorities increasingly adopt positive attitudes towards attempts to give stronger scientific and technological basis to the extension of general education. However, another factor in the development of general education which is probably of greater importance is the role of modernized general education in meeting the changing needs of preparation for entry into the labour force. The most appropriate form of preparation for the complex skill requirements of the modern economy is in fact an extended general education. Early specialization in vocational education is seen to be a less flexible and adaptive preparation for the manpower needs of industrial society than general education. Paradoxically, the increased occupational relevance of education in modern society leads to the reversal of the traditional dichotomy between general and vocational education – general education is now more related to the occupational system than early specialization. It becomes a fact of life that acquiring the skills appropriate to survival in modern society entails a general education of extended duration and the postponing of vocational specialization (Vaizey 1967).

The growth of general education and the later choice of vocational education may perform important functions for the economic system through the production of a more educated labour force and its greater flexibility in the face of occupational changes. The extension of compulsory education and the broadening of the contents of education are increasingly essential to the maintenance and growth of the production system and economic progress. There is also the possibility that general education is not only a preparation for production but also for consumption roles in modern society. It is precisely the connection between production and consumption needs which support educational trends towards more general education. Changes in the curriculum of general education suggest that it is more related to the maintenance of the organized production system than to the development of personal capacities. This contributes to the development of a form of general education stressing the introduction of new knowledge and skills which enable people to be more effectively integrated in the social system by their increased capacities for adapting to technological change. The economic production system increasingly determines the criteria of general education and the emphasis on scientific and technological subjects is seen to promote greater social stability and integration during a period of rapid technological change. However, this is not balanced in the curriculum of general education by subjects related to personal development and individual capacities for creativity and social awareness. There is a tendency in general education to overlook, or diminish the importance of those subjects which enable the individual to see himself in relation to the world and to develop capacities to act creatively in that world. This emphasis on the utilitarian purposes of general education systematically reduces its role in providing meaningful understanding of social reality. The new permutation of general education becomes a process of acquiring formal understanding of the world supporting the school and reflecting the orientation to reality of dominant economic and political groups in society. The output of general education takes the form of mental skills and knowledge external to the individual which are instrumental in the technical rational sense (Young 1971). General education imposes the dominant view of reality and reduces those capacities essential to reflecting about that dominant reality. When general education takes on the role of generating rational behaviour in a utilitarian orientation to reality, it fails to produce those critical capacities essential to relating knowledge to its social purposes. This may result in the repression of knowledge and skills which are not functional in a technical sense and which may be used to look critically at dominant social institutions. The capacity of critical awareness is more likely to arise from informal cultural agencies rather than the school, if it does arise at all. The development of this manipulative form of general education does little to influence the unequal distribution of knowledge and skills in modern society. It reinforces the use of knowledge and skills in the interests of dominant social groups, and prevents their translation into the context of problems and needs for understanding of social reality for less privileged social groups (Holley 1971).

CONCLUSION

The confrontation of educational ideologies is the centre of the "future of education" debate. The solution of basic educational problems may challenge the nature of present society. The European countries, both the enlarged "Community" and Eastern Europe, are moving towards mass education in an advanced industrial and urban form of social organization. This development poses new and challenging questions. The increase in educational provision in these countries has brought to the forefront basic questions about the social purposes of education, although this has been achieved more by the immobilism and backward thinking of educational authorities than by the vision of the so-called radicals. There is a strong tendency towards technocratic redirecting of educational systems to economic growth needs and the training of new élites (Drouard 1972). However, the realization of the scope of the crisis in modern society, which is especially evident in our educational problems, is emerging very slowly and reluctantly among authorities. Those responsible for finding radical solutions to the fundamental contradictions continue to believe that a combination of more extensive schooling and economic growth will provide the answers. Such efforts to ameliorate the situation only tend to obscure the nature of the basic problems. If European educational systems are to avoid increased technocratic control the essential political questions have to be dealt with in the near future. The necessary social and political decisions arise from the contradictions in present and future social and educational development in relation to the equality/inequality issue. The resolution of these contradictions in the future suggests a number of social and educational images determined by different views as to what we think about society as it is, as we think it will be, and as we hope it will be. It may be vital that "Those who wish not only to fit in with the future, but also to participate in it, need to understand what is at stake – the 'issues beneath the issues'..." (Harman 1972). The social issues beneath the issues of future education essentially concern the distribution of power and resources between identifiable groups in society. The interests of these groups, powerful and powerless, are the basis of alternative strategies of educational provision, and it is the conflict between these groups in the present which is the basis of future developments. Thinking about the future can only begin and end with action in the present, whether to confirm the present or change the future.

CHAPTER 3

ALTERNATIVE SOCIAL FUTURES AND SOCIAL DYNAMICS

While it may be obvious that the future of European society will emerge from the dynamics of the present constellation of development patterns in these countries, we cannot assume a priori their necessary convergence. Industrialization and technological development may be possible with significant differences in the social structure, such as political processes and the allocation of status (Birnbaum 1970). The enumeration of the characteristics of industrial society, in some prognosed post-industrial society, can attribute to it an internal coherence and uniformity that it does not possess. The economic and technological development of present society may not necessarily produce the convergence of social and political systems often suggested. Indeed, these developments may themselves produce contradictions and problems indicative of a longer-term divergence from any unilinear evolutionary trend. If we cannot assume any single future for European society, we need to consider what the alternatives may be. What structural alternatives are conceivable and what chance of realization do they possess? (Jensen 1972).

A FRAMEWORK FOR SOCIAL FUTURES

Speculation about the future has to avoid basing its models on stereotyped and vague formulations such as "conservative", "progressive", "traditional", "radical", etc. Our own viewpoint is that alternative social futures should be considered as possible solutions to problems in present society. This approach to futures-thinking in terms of alternative models is closely related to the *Constructive Futures-thinking* or *Constructive Futurology* discussed above. The overall aim of constructive futures-thinking is to produce a number of alternative images of the future "radically contrasting in 'value commitment', in 'power structure', and thus in their priorities in the development of strategies" (Faith & Jansen 1973). These alternatives can only allow very tentative statements about the future. They are intended as frameworks for interpreting certain identified problems in the present and their possible solution in the future. In this sense they serve the purpose of clarifying present systems of values which enter into our plans for the future, and facilitate the making of decisions determining the future.

The problem we identify in the present as open to alternative solutions in the future is the unequal and equal distribution of rewards and resources to different social groups. This problem is far from being resolved and there are different views as to its long-term development (Hake 1972). Two main dimensions of social life can be suggested as the key elements of present and future social development. To the degree that alternative futures take into account both the distribution of social power and influence and the allocation of social rewards and resources they can be used to bring out the contingent nature of the existing situation and confront it with alternatives. These factors are the source of conflicts and tensions in potential social development as a result of disparities in the present situation. Thinking about alternative futures for society implies making statements about future distributions of power and rewards as decisive aspects of social relations and social structure.

Galtung provides a basic framework which can be effectively used for this analysis (1970). He uses two dimensions to distinguish the basic characteristics of social systems. One dimension seeks to distinguish whether society has collectivist or individualist characteristics, the other to distinguish the vertical or horizontal nature of society, i.e. whether there is inequality or equality. We have used this framework, in a modified form, in constructing our social alternatives. The two dimensions are seen as distinguishing the basic orientation of society and the most fundamental components of the social system. One dimension distinguishes between the individualist-collectivist allocation of power and influence in society, the other between the hierarchical (vertical) – egalitarian (horizontal) variations in the distribution of rewards. It is then possible to use these two dimensions to identify the basic elements of the social systems of potential future societies, both dimensions relating to the perpetual tension and conflict between the centre and periphery in social life (Hake 1972).

As the first step in constructing alternative futures we present these two dimensions of social organization in the form of four social futures. As in Figure 1 of the two hierarchical societies, the neo-industrial will stress the dominance of economic individualism, and the social welfare the greater role of the collective. The two other alternatives will be more egalitarian societies, the compulsory collective being characterized by its collective orientation, the voluntary collective by the promotion of egalitarian individualism.

Figure 1

	Individualist	*Collectivist*
Hierarchical	Neo-Industrial	Social Welfare
Egalitarian	Voluntary Collective	Compulsory Collective

It is necessary within this framework to have a way of describing the likely internal social structure of each alternative. What, for example, would be the structure of the economic system in the hierarchical-individualist alternative, and how would it appear in the egalitarian-collectivist alternative? Or, what will be the political structures of the hierarchical collectivist and egalitarian-individualist alternatives?

The nature of society can be described and analyzed in very different terms. We explore the development potentials of present society by using aspects of the sociological frameworks employed by Hake (1972) and Jensen (1972) to construct alternative futures of social systems. They indicate that the structure and dynamics of society can be understood in terms of the interaction of four main dimensions of social life.

These dimensions are the economic, political, communal and cultural institutions and structures of society. *Economic structures* are concerned with the means of production and distribution. We should be able to make statements about economic structures in terms of what is produced, what are the production and consumption patterns, and how is economic activity regulated?

Political structures concern the control of and participation in political processes. Second-order questions are: what are the forms of decision-making? what are the mechanisms of planning and administration? what are the patterns of political communication?

Communal Structures relate to the criteria and allocation of status in society, and organization of family systems. We could then make further statements about the types of social roles and their status differentiation, the relation between work and leisure, and the patterns of neighbourhood and family organization.

Cultural structures entail the processes of the creation and transmission of culture, i.e. values, attitudes, skills and knowledge. Second-order statements could be made about the processes of creating and maintaining values and knowledge, patterns of transmitting culture through informal and formal education, and about forms of innovation and social change.

Thus for each alternative social future we can make statements about their most probable forms of economic, political, communal and cultural structures. Consequently, we shall see the relationships between social institutions and possible distributions of power as the basis of alternative social futures. These concepts also enable us to indicate a number of fundamental disparities in the social system which are at the basis of conflicts and tensions as change occurs in these four basic dimensions of the social system.

While indicating the nature of each alternative, in terms of the characteristics of their economic, political, communal and cultural systems at the European and national levels, we are not able to say which is most likely to be realized. Our own view is that these are four possibilities with constraints grounded in the present. Their realization depends on conscious political choices, the relative power of social groups, and the interaction of these factors in the planning of the future.

HIERARCHICAL ALTERNATIVES

The consensus view on future social development tends to stress the standardizing influence of continued economic growth and technological development upon social structures. This approach emphasizes the convergence of social systems leading to social uniformity over and above national cultures and political systems. It is argued that modern societies have become more complex and exacting in their requirements, not because they are capitalist or socialist, but because they are technological societies (Reuchlin 1972). The role of the economic-technological system, as the determining agency of social development, suggests the neo-industrial model of future society. However, the dynamics of this neo-industrial model of the future are also seen as giving rise to basic problems, as economic growth continues without regard to its negative social costs. There are indications of the need for increased collective action through the political system directing attention to the concept of a social welfare model of society.

A. *Neo-Industrial Society*

The dominant view of future society is characterized by the pluralistic post-industrial model of Bell (1967) and Kahn and Briggs (1972). There is a basic assumption that social conflicts and polarization will disappear in advanced industrial societies, largely as a result of the influence of technological rationality penetrating the entire culture and becoming the dominant organizing principle of social life (Galbraith 1967). This future is a continuation of the present, with improved levels of economic growth measured by quantitative indices of national income, production, capital investment and consumption based on present growth rates. Changes in the economic and technological dimensions of society bring about changes in other social institutions which adjust to the needs and requirements placed upon them. This approach on the one hand emphasizes the continuation of the agreed value of economic growth and the stability of the social system, and on the other indicates that prevalent hierarchical aspects of society will not be questioned or changed. Such a hierarchical society based on economic and technological development will maintain the stabilization of growth values and goals towards an "abundant society". This future development implies the unchanging position of different social power groups relative to one another. In spite of the inner dynamics of the system, the structure remains the same (Jensen 1972).

Economic Structures Promote Rapid Growth

The basic character of the economic system is based on the continuation of world-wide aspirations and efforts to industrialize and modernize society. The increased application of technology to production will lead to a continued rise in the gross national product and income per head of the population, thus providing a higher standard of living measured in material consumption terms (Kahn & Wiener 1967). The majority of the labour force will be engaged in the service industries, probably approaching 80% of workers in the tertiary sector (Fourastié 1966). Rising economic aspirations in advanced societies will be the basis of expanding production, while the creation of demand will be directed to encouraging consumption patterns appropriate to higher production levels induced by new technological capacities.

This development will be characterized by the tendency to increase the gap between present industrialized societies and the developing countries – the development gap. There will be a need for extensive investment of economic resources, technological innovations and knowledge by advanced societies in the Third World, but this could well conflict with the need to extend economic growth in the former and the protection of their higher consumption levels (Myrdal 1968). The protection of national economic interests will be reflected in the continued competition and will limit the capacity of international organizations to act effectively. The development of large-scale international corporations will increase considerably, thus filling the "initiative gap" produced by the restriction of political power at the international level.

Given these basic characteristics the future of European integration can be seen as the development of a large-scale market facilitating specialized production and the international division of labour. The Western European countries will maintain their national sovereignty while promoting a number of common European decision and administrative systems for economic and financial policies. Continued divisions between Eastern and Western Europe will also encourage the relative integration of foreign affairs and military alliances within the two blocs (Jensen 1972).

Political Structures Support Private Interests

The political institutions of neo-industrial society will be relatively unchanged and there will continue to be a close relationship between economic interests and political power through the institutions of representative democracy. Political institutions will be geared to the problems of maintaining economic growth and the market system of distributing of goods and services. Legislation will support economic activity with economic pressure groups significant in political processes, especially employers and workers organizations. There is likely to be a high level consensus among established parties and pressure groups on the promotion of economic growth and the development of technological capacities (Calder 1969). There will be a relatively low level of demand for public goods and services, and individual consumers will be weakly organized. There will be low levels of direct participation in decision-structures with representative democracy prevailing. Traditional authority structures in most social institutions will be maintained (Kornhauser 1960).

The traditional institutions of representative democracy could become less effective in the face of problems arising from rapid economic and technological development. Adjustment is likely to be achieved by the growth of bureaucracy in decision-making processes, and the definition of more issues and problems as technical rather than political (Weinberg 1967). This may lead to technocratic developments, involving a partial transfer of political power to technical and specialist élites. A particular manifestation of this development will be the control of mass media of communication and the problem of privacy resulting from the wide-spread availability of personal data to private and public agencies.

The development of international political structures and political integration will be inhibited by national economic interests and the continued confrontation between economic-military power blocs in Europe. European institutions will be characterized by a lack of effective political decision-structures, the dominance of administrative organs, concern with technical problems and the role of specialists (Lefevbre 1967).

Communal Structures Based on Occupational Specialization

The system of social status and organization of the communal system will tend to reflect the basic economic structures and the growth of technological requirements (Ferkiss 1969). Patterns of social life will be largely determined by specialized occupational roles with social status defined in socio-economic terms. The continued division of labour on the basis of specialist technical qualifications will promote tendencies towards a meritocratic form of status system. Non-productive social groups such as children, youth, women and the retired, will have relatively low status in terms of social reward (Hake 1972).

The dominant form of communal organization will be the nuclear family, with a high level of emphasis upon private consumption and ownership. This privatization of communal life will stress careers and the family. Sexual roles will remain relatively differentiated into male instrumental and female expressive roles (Mead 1967). Consumption and demand for goods and services will be largely private with a low level of public demand apart from very basic large-scale investments in public services such as social welfare and education. Conspicuous consumption will form a basic element of the status system. Leisure will be interpreted as time off work, and time-filling leisure pursuits will be largely based on increasing consumption levels stressing entertainment patterns.

Cultural Structures Produce Utilitarian Knowledge and Skills

The functions of cultural institutions in neo-industrial society will be related to promoting the values, attitudes, and behaviour meeting the demands of the economic system, especially high occupational and consumption aspirations.

The dominance of economic interests will tend to emphasize the utilitarian applications of knowledge and skills. The prevailing ideology will tend to favour the application of rationality in economic organization and technological development as in social organization in general (Touraine 1969). Cognitive knowledge will become the major source of values and the integrative element of culture (Habermas 1970). There will be a vast accumulation of scientific knowledge and technological capacities which will be largely applied to productive processes and the growth of economic activity.

The problems of rapid social change and individual stress will lead to emphasis upon the integration of the individual into the dominant technological system and the need for adaptive patterns of behaviour. This will give rise to an increasing stress on social technology, and technological solutions to social problems rather than the need for changes in the social system (Helmer 1966).

Neo-industrial society will stress activism in economic and leisure activities, but not encourage political and communal activism. Consequently, there will be a high stress on the utilitarian achievement motivation directed towards occupational and consumption aspirations (MacClelland 1961).

The mass media will emphasize the capacity to communicate to nuclear family units and individuals, reducing the need for a group basis to receiving communications. Communication systems will open the individual to the influence of the media but not necessarily provide access to the media for the individual. The cultural role of the individual will be passive and receptive, rather than active participation in direct creativity. This will be a society of "spectacle" and superficial cultural innovation leading to the consumption of cultural goods and services (Bordieu & Debord 1967).

B. *Social Welfare Society*

There are signs of a growing crisis in the long-term development of growth oriented societies (Mishan 1970). The capacity of neo-industrial society to manage the short-term crises of its own development may be overtaken by its incapacity to solve its long-term problems without profound changes in the social system (The Ecologist 1972).

The assumption that society will continue to support continuous growth and sustained technological change is not guaranteed in view of less optimistic forecasts. The dangerous and possibly destructive long-term implications of continued economic and technological growth are indicative of a reconsideration of present goals and priorities (Meadows 1972). The resolution of basic social problems arising from uncontrolled economic growth suggests an increased role for the political system and the reorientation of society towards social problems through collective action (Gross 1966). The sacrifice of short-term economic growth for long-term stability may have to be pursued through preventive measures to resolve social tensions arising from social inequalities and the integration of minority groups into the mainstream of social life (Jensen 1972). The pursuit of long-term stability could lead to a concentration on the social infrastructure of public services and the general improvement of social conditions (Sauvy 1973).

Economic Structures Subject to Extensive Public Control

The essential feature of economic activity will be the control of economic activity in terms of redefined social interests and the application of a broader concept of gross national wealth in the form of gross national benefit. Control of the negative social costs of economic growth will become a major feature of economic policies, with special reference to exploitation of scarce physical resources and the pollution of the environment. Private capital interest and ownership will remain although under increased political control. Major sectors of economic activity, especially the growth industries and basic public services, will be nationalized. This suggests greater centralized control by political decision-making structures divorced from private economic interests (Janne 1970).

The emphasis on the social infrastructure will lead to a reduction in private investment and private consumption in favour of public investment and consumption. The economic surplus will be redefined as a social surplus allocated to social policy goals. The definition of more goods and services as public will lead to market allocation mechanisms being counterbalanced by new social criteria of distributing goods and services under public control (Jensen 1972).

The major reorientation of priorities for economic activity will lead to basic changes at the international level. The redistribution of wealth will support the elimination of differences in the economic and social development of Europe, especially between the north and the south, and between urban and rural areas. This will be reflected in relations with the Third World and development aid will not be linked to military assistance. Aid is given to strengthen and develop the secondary productive capacities and the internal markets of developing countries. A relative decline in east-west ideological conflicts should support joint development policies. Improved international relations will facilitate a strengthening of international agencies, thus promoting the emergence of more effective aid policies and pollution control agencies.

Political Structures Promote Social Stability

The separation of decision-making structures from private economic interests will strengthen representative democratic institutions. This enables new institutions to develop at the European level and encourages new forms of direct participation at the local level. A major development will be new forms of collective decision-making and participation promoting social integration and stability. This will be manifested in economic institutions with an extension of worker-participation in management and the vertical rotation of decision-making powers. This degree of decentralization will be balanced by a major centralization of higher-level political structures with an increased capacity of public control. These general changes produce a stronger social orientation and collective interest encouraging a greater readiness to undertake major social reforms to reduce social disparities and inequalities (Jensen 1972).

At the European level, closer forms of political integration and representative political institutions are established. These institutions are able and prepared to intervene in promoting common policies with other power blocs, and are capable of over-riding the pure economic interests of member states for social purposes. This particularly leads to altered development policies within Europe and with the Third World, greater contact with the East-European countries through trade and common social policies.

Communal Structures Seek Social Integration

The major change in communal organization will be the reduced control of the economic system in determining private patterns of behaviour. Private demand and consumption will be reduced, and private ownership will decline relative to the provision of public goods and services. This may lead to more collective ownership patterns in the communal system. There will be increased collective control to redistribute wealth and equality of opportunity. The nuclear family will also diminish in importance with limited experimentation in new communal patterns of living and the redefinition of male-female roles.

While non-occupational aspects of social life become more important, this will not basically lead to any major change in the nature of the social status system. New opportunity structures provided by social policy do not produce equality as an objective, but provide social opportunity in a status system based on merit. There will be little change in the more fundamental conditions of working-life or the stratification of the occupational structure according to the division of labour as the basis of social status. Greater integration of minority groups and the underprivileged will be pursued through improved opportunity structures in response to the concern with social inequalities as a source of social conflict.

Cultural Structures Geared to Social Problems

The major aspect of cultural life will be the need to promote and legitimize the increasing collective orientation of society. Traditional patterns of behaviour and expectations are redundant, and the significance of social concerns requires the justification of this change of values. The view of social institutions as continuously open to change and revision through "rolling reforms" imposes new burdens upon cultural institutions. It requires a more than adaptative behaviour patterns. This entails a capacity to combine a high achievement orientation with the experience of ambiguity and uncertainty of required behaviour. This requires cultural institutions able to redefine a large number of social norms and to develop new patterns of social behaviour (The Ecologist 1972).

The greater interest in social problems and the strengthening of political institutions will encourage the involvement of cultural institutions with the problems of the social infrastructure. This will give rise to greater emphasis in the orientation of science and technology towards their social impact and their capacity to deal with social problems. It will further modify the normative function of cognitive knowledge in legitimating the economic growth ideology. Political institutions will provide the basic normative definitions of problems and commitments required of cultural institutions. Built into this social welfare society is the development of cultural centralization and bureaucraticization and planning of cultural life. This tends to involve closer connections between cultural institutions and governmental agencies as the involvement of political bodies increases in economic and social problems and planning. The control of science and technology is consequently extended towards the goals of social integration and stability.

EGALITARIAN ALTERNATIVES

It is possible to argue that the next thirty years should follow the same trends as the previous thirty years. However, there is no logical reason to exclude some form of social discontinuity and a radical reorientation of the social system. Discontinuity in the direction of social development can be deduced from potential social conflicts in both of the hierarchical alternatives described above.

Problems of economic growth, industrial unrest, structural unemployment, pollution and misuse of resources are potential sources of social disruption. Discontinuity may arise from the conflict between values and interests of social groups, the increased centralization and collective orientation leading to the marginal position of disadvantaged social groups (Hake 1972). There are good reasons for believing that social differences will remain in the social welfare societies, as in the neo-industrial countries, leading to the economic, political, social and cultural disabilities of large strata of the population.

Rather than the hierarchical societies being relatively "open" and "meritocratic" considerable economic and political inequality could persist and might become the source of conflict and discontinuity. The solution of these problems in favour of marginal and peripheral groups suggests the two possible egalitarian alternatives for the future of society. The potential development of an alternative society with an egalitarian basis is complicated by the conflict between collective and individual interests. Therefore, we propose two egalitarian societies. On the one hand, a compulsory collective model emphasizing the collective orientation and the dominance of the communal structures, and on the other hand a voluntary collective model concentrating on the individual orientation of cultural institutions.

A. *Compulsory Collective Society*

The compulsory collective model is based on an advanced democracy committed to the establishment of a classless society (Visalberghi 1973). This transformation may be characterized as a movement towards a new form of socialist society in which the emphasis will shift from the economic-technological and political aspects to communal solidarity. In such a future society exploitation could be excluded from social relationships. There could be a real concern for the equalization of living and cultural conditions for all social groups. This involves a set of values and goals relating to all areas of social activity which are the opposite of the prevailing culture and social structure. While promoting widespread participation in social institutions, a relatively strong central political system would be required to reinforce collective interests and control disruptive elements of individual expression. The central control problem of this compulsory collective society would be the maintenance of equality in economic terms, while preventing individual dissimilarities evolving in the form of non-productive roles (Galtung 1970).

Economic Structures Collectively Managed

The economic and social problems of advanced societies may require a fundamental reorganization of the economic-technological system (Jensen 1972). The control and redirection of economic activity would require strong collective control and coercive measures. Collective ownership could vary from the nationalization of key industries to the complete abolition of private ownership of capital. Orientation to collective needs and the public infrastructure does not mean that gross national product or its rate of growth will decline, but be redefined to include the social costs of economic activity. This kind of society would avoid interference with technological development during the reorientation of productive capacities towards collective goals. If scientific progress were sacrificed too greatly to the egalitarian ideal, a lower standard of living could produce a conservative reaction (Visalberghi 1973). The application of technology to community oriented technical progress would increasingly lead to the expansion of social services. The individual orientation of production and consumption would become less important.

At the international level, this alternative envisages radical changes within Europe and in relations with the Third World. A federal European authority would be able to plan the economic development of the politically integrated states. This would promote the equalization of economic and technological development within Europe and encourage increased economic integration with Eastern Europe countries. Radical changes within the European countries would entail the allocation of large proportions of the social product to the developing world. The socialistic economy would lead to a real concern for the equalization of living and cultural conditions in under-developed countries. This could involve a far reaching change in international structures with partially revolutionary consequences (Jensen 1972).

Political Structures Promote Organized Participation

The main change in political institutions would be the abandonment of the present forms of parliamentary and representative democracy. It would be replaced by a number of specific functional decision systems (Jensen 1972). The principle of direct democracy could be institutionalized as the organized participation of the individual in the decision systems by which he is most affected. The productive unit would become an important basis of participation, with extensive worker control, and communal and cultural institutions would be managed according to the same principle. This is a differentiated power structure, with many units and levels of decision.

More radical forms of direct democracy and participation in decentralized decision structures will be balanced by a strong centralized control emphasizing collective interests. Coercion is directed against particularistic groups but will be only used as a temporary measure given the eventual socialization to the new culture. Anarchistic tendencies will be countered by a constructive orientation to common concerns. To designate, a technologically advanced society, in contrast to technologically primitive societies, cannot be an idyllic and permissive society (Visalberghi 1973).

Tensions will arise from conflicts of anarchical, libertarian and ludic demands with the need for changes to be rationally planned in any European classless society. A radical puritan view could be strengthened for economic and moral reasons, but this will not occur without great dissent (Visalberghi 1973). These are good reasons to expect a strong centralized authority.

Communal Structures Encourage Collective Forms

The essence of communal institutions will be the breaking down of social status differences through a reduction of occupational differentiation at the basis of inequality in incomes and consumption. It is impossible to imagine an educational structure operating on a socialist basis with democratic ideals which continues with the existing, or similar, assumptions as to the division of labour. Changes in the division of labour are not utopian in that the classless society is based on vertical polyvalence and the rotation of functions. More specifically this means the abolition of unskilled, repetitive and frustrating tasks as the life long work of certain social groups (Visalberghi 1973).

Job rotation discourages social dissimilarity through occupational specialization. The degree of vertical or horizontal job rotation would depend on the level of technological development, but require the development of skills and abilities to a far greater degree than in the hierarchical societies. The development of job rotation, including a compulsory period of low level manual work, would also function to diminish other forms of social differentiation between the sexes and age groups (Hake 1971).

Diminishing private demand and consumption patterns in favour of public demand and provision of goods and services will lead to the establishment of a social income. No longer reflecting the individual's economic product, this includes reward for social service and allows only small differentials, based more on group characteristics than individual merit (Galtung 1970).

Behaviour will be oriented to collective goals, with a low level appreciation of personal and individual preferences. This will probably lead to new patterns of communal organization and a modification of the nuclear family. Experimental forms of social organization and collective living will lead to more open and flexible systems, requiring profound engagement and commitment to the principles of collective interaction and group life.

Collective concerns and the development of group living will entail a radical change in the traditional distinction between work and leisure and its replacement by a coherent and integrated social identity embracing all socially useful functions (Galtung 1970).

Cultural Structures Promote the Group Ideology

Cultural institutions will promote group solidarity, new group patterns of behaviour and group interaction. That these will evolve slowly indicates potential problems of internalizing the necessary commitments and legitimizing the changed social order. Cultural institutions play a primary ideological role in the process of social change through the creation of a "new man" (Jensen 1972). Cultural institutions will play a key role in the social system's ideological integration. Collectively organized cultural units will create "cells of innovation" which will induce social change in a controlled way. The need will be to institute structures which are capable of maintaining a continuous politicization of technology and a questioning of the values and goals of the prevailing consensus with a cultural radicalization concerning social goals and values (Hake 1972).

Cultural institutions will play an important role in developing and legitimating the new order of society and its interpretation and explanation of reality. Major social changes require the creation of a new ideology within which the old order can be discarded and new forms of behaviour be legitimized. The close relationship of science and technology to practice will encourage a major development in the adaption of the sciences to societal and collective needs. This necessitates the creation of a new knowledge-value integrate involving the integration of cognitive knowledge and normative patterns in a new ideology.

Educational structures will be an important medium for control of the social system and a medium for developing and organizing social interaction in the interests of the social group. The new ideology requires that education must accustom young people very early in life to not only consider all those activities needed by the community as useful and dignified, but also to carry out many of them, including some that are repetitive and relatively unskilled (Visalberghi 1973).

B. *Voluntary Collective Society*

While the compulsory collective model of society represents a possible egalitarian alternative, another version of an egalitarian society is possible.

Stressing individual self-expression through a voluntary collective life in an open society this alternative is based on the creation of new forms of social interaction, increasing self-government by local communities and informal associations whose main concern will be the satisfaction of the developmental needs of the individual. Libertarian and anti-authoritarian aspects of a voluntary collective society would stress creativity and personal fulfilment rather than adaptation to integrating values and norms. Such a society will place an emphasis on the fostering of innovating and creative powers in individuals, the individual being recognized as the proper agency of reorganization.

This alternative is based on the radicalization of marginal social groups, leading to new values and cultural patterns and the emergence of new solutions to the relationship between the individual and his society (Roszack 1969). An open society will allow individuals the opportunity to shape their personalities in accordance with their own inclinations and their own choices. The tolerance of contrasting individual life-styles and diverse social groups would place a significant burden upon social control mechanisms and require a major change in the capacity of individuals to tolerate dissimilarity and inconsistency. Furthermore, the emphasis upon decentralization and self-management of communal groups does not ensure the ability to integrate high levels of technology in a decentralized society.

Economic Structures Based on Decentralized Production

A basic assumption would be an extremely advanced level of technological development. This advanced technology would be geared to the support and satisfaction of social and above all individual goals and the support of self-fulfilment. Depending on the technological level the distribution of the economic surplus could take the form of a wide distribution of free goods, with special reference to transportation, communications, education and cultural goods and services. There would be a pre-eminent concern with the prevention of pollution and ecological disturbance. Social cost-benefit analysis will form the basis of social accounting. To this degree all market systems will have been replaced by social criteria for the production and distribution of goods and services.

The concept of private ownership and capital would have completely disappeared, with the development of collective ownership and consumption. The community would provide for a wide range of goods and services depending on the level of technology achieved. While economic goods and services would be communalized, this would not entail nationalization in the traditional meaning of public ownership, nor increased centralization of control over economic activity. Advanced technologies would encourage the decentralization of production in small-scale communities and co-operatives (Galtung 1970).

While the level of technology would partly determine the degree of self-sufficiency of communal groups, there could be a number of chosen levels of technology. Providing their activities produce no mutual pollution or interference, the level of technology could vary between communities. Advanced technology as an aid to decentralization of productive and service activities would reduce the need for densely populated urban areas. Well distributed transportation systems and electronic communications would facilitate this development.

At the European level a politically integrated Europe that moves beyond centralized foıms of economic management would dominate, with the decline of national interests. The development of decentralized and self-sufficient communities would not require centralized institutions. Common problems would be the concern of short-term commissions according to the *ad hoc* principle. A similar development would have occurred in the East and West European countries, and decentralized communities cooperate in dealing with common problems including the equalization of relationship with the Third World.

Political Structures Encourage Extensive Participation

The main feature stressed is the full participation of all individuals in decisions directly affecting them, and the full representation of communal groups. Wide-spread participation in decision-making involves developing new political structures, with an emphasis on decentralization and a reduction in centralized institutions. These decentralized structures would be varied and complex, differing from community to community. The guaranteeing of individual and group rights would centre on these participation structures, and the system would tend to function through a multiplicity of decentralized self-managing groups.

A continual problem of decision structures would be defining the area where self-realization of the individual may restrict the self-realization of others. A variety of forms of political activity would be available to the individual, ranging from active involvement to complete withdrawal. The individual may withdraw from any relationship which becomes exploitive or restrictive. The decentralization of self-management communities would promote tolerance of the minorities and diversities often seen as threats to the stability society (Morin 1969).

The catalytic function of activist self-determining groups would be the contestation of hierarchical and centralization tendencies in society, and the encouragement of active involvement of the individual in self-determination and social criticism. These activist groups will play a key role in cultural radicalization, in proposing alternatives in social structures and in realizing these in concrete situations. Political consciousness of the individual would give rise to radical social action and new social forms (Debray 1967).

None of these developments necessarily negates the use of advanced technologies. Technology could provide access to information for all individuals and social groups, and provide a basis for continuous and flexible media linking participation and decision processes. The collection, storage and utilization of data would not be allowed to infringe the rights of groups and individuals, and the media of mass communication would be democratized in terms of input and access (Naville 1963).

Communal Structures with Flexible Forms of Living

The communal system would support a wide range of communal activities and groups, with individuals encouraged to seek self-realization through participation in diverse social groups. The diversity of life-styles, and the acceptance of dissimilarity and inconsistency, would be highly valued. The principle of self-realization could stress the individual's involvement in the community. A major aspect of this process might be the weakening of predetermined social roles according to racial, sexual, age and occupational criteria, thus liberating many minority and underprivileged groups. A corollary would be the capacity of the individual to leave and join diverse communal groups, and easy geographical mobility would encourage movement from community to community. This could lead to the international, multi-lingual and polycultural nature of many communities (Galtung 1970).

Change in the communal structures of society could result from wide experimentation with new patterns of communal living. A major feature would be the extensive communal provision and sharing of facilities and the breakdown of traditional patterns such as the nuclear family as a basis of ownership and consumption. Patterns of childrearing and households may become more diverse, with the growth of communal forms of living (Morin 1970). Personal relationships would become a major source of individual growth and self-realization when deprived of their legal, moral and economic basis. Changed values and attitudes in relation to technology and economic production may lead to radical forms of communal organization that undermine traditional consumption patterns (McHale 1970).

The essence of change in the communal system results from the transformation of the economic basis of social stratification. Occupational role and income would play an increasingly smaller role in social life and the egalitarian basis would promote an integrated definition of the individual's worth, including economic, political, communal and cultural capacities. To this degree horizontal polyvalency would be encouraged depending on the technological level achieved. Work will no longer be seen as opposed to leisure definition, and leisure is no longer defined as time off from labour. There will be an emphasis upon tailoring economic roles to fit the individual's needs and interests balanced against collective needs. The compulsory rotation of economic functions could be regarded as restricting the individual's freedom. Choice of a life-long economic function would be possible if the individual so chooses, since this does not determine the broader social role of the individual. A basic income would be guaranteed to every individual depending on the technological level of his particular self-governing community (Galtung 1970).

Cultural Structures Support Innovation and Creativity

The nature of the cultural institutions would be dominated by the encouragement of self-realization through participation in communal activities. The process of developing new cultural forms arises from the stress on self-affirmation. The promotion of equality is achieved through the real and continuing process of cultural politicization and questioning of values and knowledge leading to cultural action and the redefinition of social reality (Freire 1970).

Cultural institutions would be required to support a wide range of communal activities and the creative and innovative capacities of individuals. This would require the support of diverse value systems. Great importance would be given to capacities of tolerance and the acceptance of inconsistency and diversity in life-styles as central to the development of the individual and the propensity for active self-expression. The stress on self-knowledge and consciousness suggests the significance of the exploration of the individual's sense of self and the mechanisms of expanding self-awareness (Laing 1967). Culture will become a process of creating the understanding and meaning of reality, and social action will become its creative dimension. Such a society would democratize culture for all individuals and groups and could link cultural expression to the aspirations of all social groups in a permanent process of social activity and creativity. Emphasis will be given to cultural creation, the democratization of culture and the relation of culture to everyday life, and stress the *joie de vivre* associated with festivity and creative cultural expression (Neville 1970).

Although the ludic and spontaneous expression contribute to the creative dimensions of social action, cognitive forms of understanding would not lose their significance. There would be a stress upon the reflexive nature of knowledge, relating it to values in the form of a new knowledge-value integrate. Cognitive knowledge would be considered as supportive of personal and social awareness. Forms of knowledge would lose the rigidity of their traditional hierarchy, and emphasize the adequacy of facts and conceptual categories to the understanding and interpretation of social experience. The uses of knowledge and technologies would be closely associated with the development of solutions to recognized problems, and the needs of social creativity and invention (Willener 1970).

Criteria of objectivity would be questioned against reflection upon institutionalized meanings and interpretations of reality. Reflective knowledge is interpreted as the source of radical contestation in society and social action. Science and technology are not antipathetic towards the objectives of personal and social emancipation and are seen as beneficial and liberating. Technology, in particular, will be redirected towards humanistic and personal ends. The use of science and technology could become a play with the emerging potentialities of the socially emancipated and involved individual in the transformation of social reality (Marcuse 1969).

CONCLUSION

Our analysis has led us to outline two main trends in the future of social development. On the one hand, the trend towards an hierarchical society stressing either economic or political goals on the other hand, towards a more egalitarian society stressing either communal or cultural goals. We have suggested the basic features of the individual and collective tensions in social development in terms of four alternative futures for society and sketched the outline of their possible economic, political, communal and cultural structures and processes. Although it is not our task to make a choice between these alternatives on the basis of our own values, we have indicated some of the factors of tension and stress which may suggest certain developmental tendencies in the future. Nevertheless, the future should be guided by conscious choice between alternatives, and the social planning processes should be aware of the possibilities and constraints of possible alternative choices for future society. If the alternatives presented here serve the function of illuminating the long-term consequences, the images of society in the year 2000, of present value system and priorities in social planning, we feel that this could lead to open-mined and meaningful discussion of the most desirable future and the subsequent consideration of strategies to achieve that future. The future remains a question of political decision.

CHAPTER 4

TOWARDS ALTERNATIVE FUTURES FOR EDUCATION – EDUCATIONAL STRUCTURES AND PROCESSES

The meaning of any hypothesis about the development of any sector of society, such as education, depends on the framework provided by the development of society in general. This is especially the case when the variables considered depend upon social and political possibilities and constraints. We need a way of analyzing the relationships of society with education in order to identify those social factors which influence the nature of educational systems, especially the allocation of resources to and within the educational system.

We have tried to construct a framework containing the factors deemed most relevant and of interest in their present structure, and then questioned how these might develop in the future. On the basis of such an analysis it is possible to project the social-educational relationship as possible futures of the social-educational system. The analysis of past and present structures and processes may allow the tentative presentation of some statements about its development and dynamics. The general social factors presented as alternative social futures indicate the range, or sets, of possibilities for possible structures and processes in education in the future.

In terms of educational variables, we suggest those factors which highlight the major developments most likely in the different social systems suggested in Chapter 2. By constructing alternative educational futures we can say that the future could be so, and by assessing the requirements of their realization contribute to meaningful reflection on the goals and values of educational policy.

Alternatively futures for education are only of value when actually used for planning and ultimately transformed into political measures. Only within a comprehensive long-term framework can decisions be subjected to adequate analysis of their social motivation and consequences. It is in order to avoid arbitrary and irrational formulation of short-term measures that a long-term prospective framework is necessary.

In long-term speculation an effort is made to break away from the ideas which contemporary trends suggest and to consider possible changes in social objectives and priorities in education. There is a serious danger in short-term planning that concern with familiar and present problems and dilemmas prevents any consideration of possibilities beyond contemporary trends in political and ideological solutions to conflicts of interest in educational development. It may in fact be more risky to assume that the most pronounced contemporary trends will be perpetuated than to engage in longer term speculation of an explicitly normative nature. Moreover, short and long-term speculation have important functional links. Long-term speculation can influence short-term thinking by making it more open-ended through presenting it with a wider perspective. Possibilities for the long-term future can make us more aware of contemporary choices and values. It can offer new reflections upon solutions to present problems and policies and promote more effective planning and strategies which are "future-forming" in social and educational terms. Conversely, short-term speculation of concrete strategies is important to long-term thinking in the sense that short-term planning forms the step towards achieving the desired future state in the long-term. Short-term planning becomes the process of making concrete the realization of the future in the present.

This type of long-term social and educational planning is only slowly beginning to emerge (Alberta 1972). Unfortunately, it is safer and more comfortable for present power groups in education to add to or subtract from what already exists than to engage people in effective long-term planning which is future oriented in an open way (Kyöstiö 1972). We acknowledge that any statement of future possibilities and alternatives by ourselves can be only of indirect relevance. The alternatives we offer can at the most provide a general perspective on future social and educational policies that may illustrate the general significance of possible points of departure for present education towards the future. When future trends in education are presented they should not be taken as forecasts which will be realized as such. They represent only some of the developmental tendencies which can be structured in very different forms. There can be no question of the alternatives presented being any more than indications of the potential consequences of innovative ideas which may function for development in different directions.

We undertook our construction of alternative futures for the educational system by analyzing the educational dimensions of the social alternatives in terms of four dimensions: educational aims and goals, educational structures, educational processes and educational resources. We considered these dimensions to be most significant and relevant to the discussion of strategies.

The alternative social systems proposed will have implications for any particular institutional area of future society. The dominant values and goals of society lead to the definition of the situation of education in the social system. The alternative social futures, suggested in Chapter 3, indicate a) how the definition of the situation of education will be influenced by different values and goals, and b) how its relationships with other social dimensions will be regulated. We try to indicate how the goals of education are socially contingent and dependent on the dominant sectors of the social system such as economic or political interests. We ask two major questions about educational goals. On the one hand, "what is the main social reference point for the determination of the knowledge and values which education is intended to produce?", and "which behavioural aptitudes is education expected to produce?". Answers to these questions suggest the nature of the world orientations of individuals and social groups which are produced by educational processes. By world orientation we mean the ways in which the social/physical environment is experienced, perceived and responded to. The world orientation supported in each alternative will determine how individuals and social groups are expected to contribute to the development and change of the social and physical world (Van den Berg & Postma 1971).

In relation to the structures of education, we considered five basic factors in the provision of educational facilities in possible education strategies. These related to the emphasis given to formal and informal education; the structure of formal education with particular reference to patterns of differentiation, and the relation between provision for youth and adult groups in the population; the distribution of educational facilities in relation to regional needs; the structure and distribution of decision-making powers in education systems; and the specific nature of systems for the guidance and counselling of learners in relation to educational provision. It is an open question as to whether the discussion of educational structures may cloud constructive thinking about the processes of education. In the longer term it may be that educational structures should be subordinate to the definition of educational processes. This was a contentious question within our own group and we return to it in Chapter 4 in considering educational change.

In discussing and analyzing teaching-learning processes or pedagogical practices we simplified a very complex theoretical analysis into five major variables relating to learning objectives, educational content and activities, teaching-learning strategies and media employed. Patterns of decision-making, already discussed in terms of educational structures, are seen in terms of curriculum development covering the definition of learning objectives, contents, interaction strategies and media employed in learning. The planning of a teaching-learning process in a curriculum is seen primarily as a problem of the definition of objectives, or qualifications, to be generated by learning. Secondly we examined the defined contents and types of learning activities likely to produce the desired qualifications. Both these qualifications and contents are seen as determined by desired world orientations to be produced by educational processes.

The patterns of interaction strategies between learners and learning resources were investigated as the third and fourth aspects of learning processes. On the one hand, we examined the interaction between learners and formal resources within the school, such as teachers, and on the other hand the interaction between the school and the community, that is between formal and informal resources of learning. As the fifth aspect of the learning process we looked at the nature of the technologies to be employed in the learning process – a question of the media used to produce desired learning objectives and relating equally to interaction within the school and between the school and the community.

It will be obvious that different solutions to the foregoing problems of educational aims, structures and pedagogical processes have major implications for the allocation of resources to the educational system and the through-put of the system in terms of student flows and outputs. In considering the demands of the educational system upon economic resources we distinguished the micro-economic and macro-economic aspects of the problem of resources. At the micro-economic level we questioned the trends, or flows, in the number of students, qualified graduates, and teachers and other personnel. Secondly, we asked how these follows will influence demands on resources in terms of buildings and equipment, i.e. in capital investments. The capital and current expenditure requirements of the preceding projections are employed, thirdly, to indicate how the costs of education as a percentage of public expenditure and Gross National Expenditure might develop in the future. On the basis of these considerations we asked, fourthly, what might be the potential sources and means of financing the educational system in the future. In practice, we found that the estimation of student flows, the requirement upon resources, the costs and the means of financing the various policies proposed to be nonexistent in the long term. We draw considerably upon the forecasts made in one important report as these relate to the various alternatives proposed (Jensen 1972).

The macro-economic issues relate very closely to the more general problems of the nature of future society and the orientation of education, therefore we discuss them in the appropriate sections of the other chapters. The problems raised at the macro-economic level relate equally to the social-economic relationship, the definition of educational goals and the qualifications required from the educational process. The kind of questions raised at the macro-economic level, questions of political economy in traditional terms, were respectively: will education be primarily geared to economic and manpower demand? What are the overall trends in economically required qualifications produced? what specific qualifications are required? and if education is geared to non-economic demands, what might be the economic consequences?

On the basis of the social background presented in Chapter 2, we consider educational goals, structures, processes and resources for each alternative, in constructing four alternatives for the future of educational development.

We wish to stress that we consider all four alternatives to be inherent in the present structure of European societies as development possibilities. To the extent that these alternatives are based on the objective characteristics of social and educational systems, the existing structures are confronted with possible alternatives implying a stabilization or change of present conditions. Although we shall discuss some issues of the tensions and dynamics involved in the alternatives suggested, they are intended to represent alternatives rather than stages of development of European social and educational systems. Consequently, we leave the choice between them and the development of strategies appropriate to their realization as open possibilities for others to determine.

PART I: EDUCATION IN THE HIERARCHICAL ALTERNATIVES

The optimism of the recent expansionist period in European educational systems forms the image of the future educational system. The emphasis on modifying educational structures lead some to propose that future educational systems will be characterized by the extension of pre-school education, the virtual generalization of secondary education to the age of 18, and an extensive expansion of post-compulsory education (Poignant 1973).

These projections of educational structures into the future provide limited definition of the alternative educational systems possible. Others stress changes in the curriculum, teaching methods and uses of educational technology (Reuchlin 1972). There can be little doubt that educational decision-makers will pay greater attention to more rational curriculum development and efficient teaching methods in response to the knowledge explosion, technological developments and changing channels of communication. There is a growing consensus that these features will be increasingly important aspects of forward-looking schools in the next decades (IBE 1970).

Together, the change in structures and new educational processes form the basis of the two alternative educational systems to be outlined here. On the one hand, the orientation of education to the economic system and manpower requirements in neo-industrial society lead to a minimum definition of the future as an extension of present trends in educational policy. This alternative is clearly a projection of present trends. On the other hand, the extreme limit of the extension of formal education in the future, is clearly indicated in the social welfare alternative. This model concentrates on the social need and demand for education and the political orientation of education in promoting social integration. The essential question remains as to whether these trends promise a radical qualitative change in educational systems, or are rather incremental additions to the present system through increasing its external and internal efficiency.

A. *Neo-Industrial Education*

Educational Goals

The social orientation of education will be towards the development of economic and technological growth. This will be achieved through the development of knowledge and skills appropriate to production and consumption capacities. A basic premise of educational strategies will be the development of the inherent and unequal abilities of individuals according to the requirements of the complex occupational structure. Rapid economic and technological progress will increasingly render skills obsolete and demand new capacities, and education will be largely geared to overcoming these changes in the occupational structure through promoting flexible and adaptive capacities (Reuchlin 1972).

This will be particularly clear at the level of adult education which is closely connected to economic demands and takes the form of retraining or "recyclage". Students' abilities and aspirations are mobilized in relation to the manpower needs of the economic and technological systems. The distribution of opportunities is based on the pyramid of differences in measured ability, and social barriers to equal educational opportunity do not undermine the selective and allocative functions of education. Consequently, education will tend to support the hierarchical aspects of society, the prevailing values of production and consumption, and the integration of individuals into an adaptive and individualist ethos.

The promotion of talent and ability through education will lead to a concentration on the cultivation of intellectual and cognitive capacities. These capacities of cognitive rationality will be guided by the predominant demands for economic and technical instrumentality. Preserving the established economic and political system entails the production of the minimum knowledge and skills necessary to the maintenance of an efficient and stable social system, and non-development of those capacities leading to reflection upon the social and personal significance of learning and educational qualifications.

Educational Structures

An important characteristic of educational structures will be the emphasis upon formal structures of education. Formal is understood as a specialized milieu in which to learn knowledge and skills. There would be little attention given to informal learning situations outside the school, and school would prepare for informal social situations such as private life, consumption and leisure. The use of advanced educational technologies, such as audio-visual media, would facilitate individualized learning (Reuchlin 1972). However, the learning process would remain formal in the sense that hierarchical didactical processes are involved, and the learner is seen as a consumer of standardized products.

There might be a significant development of private agencies of education, but this would not entail informal learning in the broader sense. These private institutions would be predominantly oriented to economic and technological demands upon education. Education would play an increasing service role for productive units. Industry would take a strong interest in education with a vocational emphasis and the level of adult education would be increasingly organized by industrial firms, probably in new industry-sponsored agencies. (OECD 1971a).

The structure of formal education would follow main trends in present policies. Pre-school provision would be expanded with special emphasis towards children of the lower social economic classes, the objective being to promote their cognitive and linguistic skills relative to the demands of the formal school system. This is guided by the basic need to promote all available talent, and the achievement standards of a school system based on cognitive skills (OECD 1971b).

The distinctions between primary and secondary education will be abolished in basic schooling to the compulsory school leaving age, and the gradual introduction of differentiation within comprehensive schools at the lower secondary level. A "common core curriculum" will provide the selective device with options providing for different talents and intellectual levels at the secondary level. The compulsory period of general education will be generalized towards 17/18 years of age, although differentials will probably remain between northern and southern European countries. Vocational specialization will begin in the upper secondary cycle, probably in new upper secondary schools. Attendance ratios will probably reach the 80%-90% level in the last two years (Poignant 1973).

The tertiary level will probably take the form of a binary system, consisting of universities for purely academic courses and polytechnics offering more applied courses. The latter will be especially concerned with the provision of post-experience short courses of occupational relevance. The enrolment ratios in full-time higher education will reach the 30-35% level, and will follow directly upon completion of secondary school.

Recurrent education will be provided through private facilities in industrial enterprises, and will be closely geared to vocational needs, industrial re-training, and on-the-job training. Financial support for adult education would be restricted to vocationally oriented courses supported by industrial enterprises. There would be limited public provision of facilities for adult education related to general and individual interests. Such adult educational provision represents a minimal definition of permanent education, as an addition to the unchanged structures, geared to providing a "second chance" (Janne 1972).

Regional disparities in educational provision, and the distribution of educational resources, would continue to be a major problem. The lack of adequate regional development policies in terms of community development programmes would encourage rural-urban migration within and between countries, and this would be reflected in the perpetuation of major educational differentials (Borelli 1972). The large-scale nature of educational institutions, especially at the upper secondary and tertiary level, would continue to favour urban areas, which facilitate small geographical catchment areas.

The structure of educational decision-making will respond to improved educational planning relating the flow of students and occupational requirements through improved manpower planning. A relatively centralized planning system will relate increased social demand for education with economic needs, and the initial rapid expansion of higher education will be increasingly controlled on the grounds of costs. This may involve the introduction of the *numerus clausus* on a wide scale to avoid underemployment of graduates. Within educational institutions the traditional hierarchical structures of decision-making will be little modified, especially in relation to objectives. Recognition of interest groups will take the form of integration through consultative machinery.

Structures of guidance and counselling will be strongly related to the pyramid of abilities and manpower needs. Guidance will continue to play a function in adapting individual abilities to the labour market. The role of counselling will be a selective one, leading to the allocation of individuals to academic and vocational options and tracks at later stages. The emphasis will be the objective assessment of individual differences in terms of measured cognitive abilities (Cicourel & Kituse 1963).

Educational Processes

The nature of curriculum development, i.e. decision-making about objectives, contents, interaction strategies and media will be seen as technical questions for education authorities. The individual will be the consumer of predetermined and centralized educational programmes. Choice will be limited to available programmes. Individualization could lead to a significant reduction in the group nature of education and the increased control capacities of providers of learning systems (Gagne 1965).

The objectives of educational processes will emphasize the integration of the individual into the hierarchical social system, the productive process and consumption patterns. Adaptation will be more important than creativity and the cognitive domain will dominate learning objectives with emphasis upon the cultivation of abstract intellect capacities (Bloom 1971).

Contents and activities of the educational programme will emphasize scientific and applied technical knowledge and skills relating to control over the physical environment. Natural and technical sciences will predominate over social studies. The curriculum at the secondary and tertiary level would be divided between cumulative and non-cumulative courses, the former performing a selective function for further education. The exact sciences are seen as cumulative and organized on a unit basis, while the social sciences and humanities are non-cumulative. Consequently, the emphasis upon non-reflexive exact sciences will reduce the critical content of education (Goodlad 1967).

The stress on the achievement motive will encourage interaction strategies based on competitiveness within educational institutions. The educational process will continue to be controlled by the teacher, as expert in his discipline, and the control dimension of learning (Young 1971). This will apply in youth and adult education in that learning is a closed system with predetermined objectives. The application of advanced technologies to the individualization of instruction will encourage the atomization and competitive nature of learning. The close relation between educational qualifications and selection will support this individualism and competitiveness at all levels including adult education with its vocational orientation (Skinner 1968).

The formalized and individualized nature of the learning process will determine the restricted interaction with the non-school environment. Centralization and institutionalization of the learning process lead to a reduced interaction with social agencies. Non-school learning will be encouraged only on a very selective, adaptive and impersonal basis, reflecting the basic orientation of education to production and consumption functions. There will be a low level interaction with non-economic agencies capable of promoting the association of learning with social relevance.

Such a system of education could employ a wide range of learning technologies and media. The basic economic orientation of society will encourage rapid developments of educational technologies, including hard- and software. The use of media for the purposes of individualizing instruction would increase the control over learning processes and manifest a trend to the learner's being defined as a consumer rather than a creator. Educational technologies could represent an increase of central control by undermining the collective nature of learning (Oettinger 1968).

Educational Resources and Finance

A general trend in student numbers at all levels of education, but especially at the upper secondary cycle, the tertiary and, to a lesser extent, in adult education follows partly from the improved retentive capacities of the lower secondary cycle, the legislative extension of the upper secondary cycle, and a consequent increase at the tertiary level. Pre-school provision will be expanded considerably. The almost total enrolment of the appropriate age groups is assumed for the compulsory period of schooling to age 17/18 and a 30-35% enrolment in higher education. The most significant change will be in adult education, given its orientation to purely vocational needs. It can be estimated that if one-sixth of working time is devoted to adult education, then the adult student population will be more than twice that of students in ordinary full-time tertiary education. It should be noted that this is a conservative estimate based on the purely vocational nature of this education. Some estimates are to be found in the table below.

TABLE: *Estimates of the Adult "Student" Population compared to the Number of Students at the Tertiary Level.*

Selected Countries, in the year 2000

	Economically Active Population (25 years and over[a])	*Adult "Student" Population (in full time equivalents[a])*	*Number of Students[a] the Third Level[b]*
France	19.352.300	3.225.400	1.400.400
Germany, F.R.	23.901.100	3.983.500	1.470.300
Italy	19.137.300	3.189.500	1.496.700
The Netherlands	5.141.700	856.900	395.400
Sweden	3.234.000	539.000	208.800
United Kingdom	24.005.900	4.000.000	1.601.100

Sources: [a] Schwietert, A., Nahr, W.: Westeuropa 1985 *op. cit;*
[b] Jensen's estimates.

The trend in the number of educational personnel will be influenced by conflicting tendencies. The replacement of teachers by new educational technologies would be offset by the development of new educational roles especially in the expansion of counselling services. Expansion of adult education will also influence teacher requirements. The ratio of teachers per 100 students will probably reach 7% for the first and second levels and 13% for higher education (Jensen 1972).

The provision of building and *equipment* will depend on new patterns of multiple usage of educational institutions. This will not be highly significant in this system. The rationalization of building techniques, with industrialized building methods based on standardized and pre-fabricated elements, will become important. The emphasis on high-cost technologies in education and commercially produced learning systems and packages would probably increase capital investment considerably, and possibly delay their introduction on a wide scale (Hake 1973). The optimistic view of costs suggests that a reduced birth rate and new technologies will reduce the impact of the costs of expanded education. The rapid expansion of the tertiary level will entail a rapid growth of expenditures at this level relative to primary and secondary education. Secondary education will tend to take precedence over primary education, but will compete strongly with pre-school provision. There will be a distinction between the financing basis of public and private education. Public education will be financed by public funds through the system of taxation and public expenditures, especially at the primary and secondary level. The rapid expansion of the costs of higher education will be offset by the probable introduction of a loan-basis of financing students. The loans will be repayable in relation to the growth of the individual's earned income over a period of 15 to 20 years. Adult and vocational education will be partly or exclusively financed by industrial enterprises, with non-vocational adult education receiving little or no public support.

B. *Social Welfare Education*

Educational Goals

Education is based on the overall goal of reducing basic inequalities in social and educational opportunities. Education is seen as the major agency for promoting greater opportunity and individual social advancement. There will be an emphasis on the achievement motivation with the diffuse pressures of failure no longer ascribed to social factors and educational barriers. There will be a redirection of education towards the maximum promotion of talents and abilities through educational systems (OECD 1971c).

The social reference point of educational strategies is modified by the realization that education serves not only to produce economically useful knowledge and skills. This leads to new educational policies related to the needs basic to the solution of social problems and the promotion of social stability. Education becomes closely geared to the needs of social integration, and the inclusion of disadvantaged and underprivileged groups in the social and educational infrastructure. Education comes to be viewed as a social right, and duty, of the citizen, enabling him to contribute his maximum capabilities to the solution of collectively defined social problems. Capacities of flexibility and adaptability to changing economic and social demands will be stressed in education (Husén 1972).

A major goal will be to compensate on a broad scale for socially determined inequalities in modes of expression and learning capacities, and to raise the levels of general educatability in the population. This is achieved, not only by "cognitive gain" intervention strategies at the pre-school level, but by strategies seeking to influence attitudes toward education. These developments seek to reduce the social and emotional distance between lower socio-economic groups and the educational system, and will be institutionalized as lifelong intervention strategies in the form of recurrent education (Bengtsson 1971).

The social problem orientation of education will lead to development of social skills, and especially capacities for group work and capacities for cooperation. This may lead to symbolic and integrationist attitudes and norms. Cognitive knowledge of social problems would be encouraged with a high stress on the performance standards of good citizenship. This would be a complement to, and extension of, the emphasis on technical rationality and cognitive skills related to the economic system which are relatively unchanged. Vocational education would be strongly complemented by general education at all levels, and a balanced integration of intellectual, social and affective capacities would be encouraged. More effective social and emotional flexibility in a changing society would be the long-term goal, thus reducing social conflict and promoting social stability (Holley 1971).

Educational Structures

The emphasis on a centralized collective power, would emphasize the formal educational system and a general priority for public education as opposed to private education. The concentration on formal, public education would mean a relatively low level concern for informal education and the "parallel school". Indeed, the formal school system would be seen as a preparation for informal learning, with a broader orientation to capacities of dealing with social and political problems. The formal institutions will be seen as a collective means of controlling and manipulating informal sources of learning. This reflects the public and political functions of education in the social welfare society. The extent of private education will be restricted to purely vocational education at the adult level, and will play a smaller role in the overall educational system.

In the structure of formal education there will be significant extensions of public educational provision. Pre-primary education will be important and its generalization will call for a large increase in facilities and resources. It will retain its largely formal character despite the greater emphasis upon social education and the development of social and affective skills.

The primary and secondary levels will be integrated in the basis school, or *école unique*, to the age of 16. The upper secondary stage will be increasingly integrated in comprehensive institutions providing general and vocational education. Compulsory education will be extended to 18 or 19 years, with full-time attendance as the general practice, although there may be work experience and social service programmes for less able students. The comprehensive schools will provide common courses, especially in the socially-oriented elements. A strong element will be optional programmes of individualized instruction in cognitive subjects, and ability grouping as a general practice in non-social courses (Janne & Géminard 1973).

Post-secondary education will be largely concentrated in the comprehensive form of higher education linking general and professional preparation. There will be a distinction between long and short general education, and full-time higher education will tend to follow immediately after the secondary school. Permanent education will commence at the post-secondary level and will be extended considerably in its general education dimensions. Unqualified adults will be enabled to attend university courses of general education, and new general education facilities may be provided on the basis of new technologies and media such as the Open University (Simpson 1972). However, adult vocational education will remain the domain of private education institutions sponsored by industry, but not providing any general education, which is the domain of public education. The post-secondary system will be based on the credit, or units, system, enabling fulltime and part-time students to build up qualifications for jobs and further study (Schwartz 1974).

Regional policies in the distribution of educational facilities and resources would emphasize the redressing of regional disparities. Special emphasis would be given to urban-rural differentials in educational achievement. Integrated regional development politices would relate educational provision to broader social criteria of equity and equality. A significant feature of such policies would be the linking of educational facilities at different levels in the form of the educational district – *district scolaire* – providing educational facilities for a specific area and including general cultural and sporting facilities (Schwartz 1974).

Decision-making in education will be characterized by a mixture of centralization and decentralization. General objectives of educational policy, the determination of priorities and the global distribution of resources will be determined at the central level. While expertise will play an important role in determining overall objectives and planning, there will be indirect representation of educational pressure groups in consultative bodies. Centralized bodies will only determine broad and general guidelines. Decentralization will take the form of delegation of specific decisions to the educational district authority, e.g. allocation of the global budget, curriculum, and appointment of teachers and other personnel. Interest groups within the district will be indirectly represented in governing bodies, but there will be little initiative at the school or instructional level. Within the individual institution, participation will be predominantly integrative and symbolic and will take the form of joint consultation and advisory functions.

The structures performing guidance and counselling functions will be extended. There will be a change from synchronic to diachronic guidance stressing the continuous and permanent nature of the guidance function (Visalberghi 1973). Guidance facilities would be available throughout the system of permanent education. The emphasis on vocational guidance and counselling would be reduced by the greater orientation to the social and affective dimensions of education. Counselling in personal and social problems would gain in importance, and the significance of flexible and adaptive qualities in individuals would lead to the development of new guidance personnel categories. Guidance and counselling agencies would also be responsible for containing the stress and frustrations engendered by the emphasis on achievement and the rapidly changing nature of the social system (Reuchlin 1972).

Educational Processes

The nature of decision-making in teaching-learning processes reflects the centralization-decentralization dimensions. The technical approach to educational processes will be reflected in a relatively closed system of education in which learning objectives are determined at the central level, while choice of media and interaction strategies are determined at the educational district level. The role of commercial production of learning materials will be restricted. Publicly controlled research and development will predominate in curriculum development and new learning systems. The use of high cost technologies in individualized learning systems could encourage centralized development programmes.

Learning objectives would stem from the balance between vocational and general education, and the qualifications generated will relate equally to vocational and social requirements. At all levels of education the balanced and integrated development of intellectual and social capacities would be encouraged. This integrated approach to learning objectives can be best seen as "mastery learning" in which learners are helped to develop the basic skills necessary for the further learning required of them, thus enabling them to learn independently "learning how to learn" (Visalberghi 1973).

General education will stress the basic operational "languages" or methods of learning. The mastery approach to learning will stress a structured approach to learning with concentration on the basic structures of different bodies of knowledge (Ford & Pugno 1964). This will lead to the predefinition of objectives and the breaking down of learning programmes into units – *système des unités capitalisables*. The specification of the unit approach to learning programmes will be sequential, but each unit can be capitalized in the sense that it produces clearly defined skills or knowledge (Schwartz 1974).

At all levels there will be a balance in general education between the exact sciences and mathematics, the social sciences, languages, and practical activities. Adult general education will tend to stress the problems of the learners in their social and political milieu, thus reflecting the basic orientation of education towards collective concerns.

Social sciences will form a major component of the common core throughout education, and also be available as a specialized option. Emphasis will be placed on social education for social skills. Language education will concentrate on the development of oral language skills, with an early introduction of foreign languages alongside the mother tongue. Practical activities will relate to the development of manual skills, aesthetic education, artistic expression and creativity. Emphasis will be given to the use and manipulation of materials and tools in the areas of music, drama, plastic arts, and sport. These will gain in emphasis at the secondary level, and will be available as a specialized option in general education as well as the common core.

Interaction strategies within educational institutions will become more complex with the adjustment of study courses to individual abilities and needs. Concern for the affective development of the individual and his integration in the social group will lead to the need for carefully planned group activities stressing the development of group oriented behaviour. Interaction strategies as a whole will be largely characterized by new patterns emphasizing the importance of non-graded instruction and team-teaching. Learning will occur in different size groups according to its purposes. Individualization will enable units to be adjusted to specific needs and abilities of individual pupils and will concentrate on cognitive learning. The common core curriculum will be characterized by mixtures of large group learning for the transmission of common information, and smaller working groups in laboratory classes and work areas for more closely guided small group study and practical activities (Shaplin & Olds 1964). The traditional classroom will disappear in the "open-plan school" facilitating a multiplicity of groupings and activities.

The new role of the teacher in guiding the learner between the units available in common and optional programmes, and providing assistance on methods of work within units, will reduce the function of the teacher as the major learning resource and a multitude of learning materials and resources will be available (Rée 1970). This will probably increase the significance of the teacher's role as animator of learning. Guided choice by students will be limited to choice of units, methods of learning, and the speed of work within the predetermined compulsory and optional programmes with pre-set objectives. The development of cumulative units will assist the development of self-assessment. Continuing general education for adults will strongly reflect the social purposes of education developed in the compulsory school. Small group discussion and interaction will be encouraged, emphasizing group education – *l'éducation mutuelle*. This is based on common problems in social and political life and is followed by group evaluation and reinforcement of group identification (Schwartz 1974).

Interaction strategies with the non-school environment will be influenced by the orientation to social life. The opening up the relationship of the school with its social environment will stress the manipulation of non-school factors through educational provision. The school will provide the means of coming to terms with social and personal problems and encouraging group integration. The community will be encouraged to support educational goals, and parents will be able to participate in school management and educational activities. Multiple use of school facilities will encourage community participation in the life of the institution, including youth and adult cultural and sport facilities. Professional education at the post-secondary level will take the form of full-time training interspersed with periods of practical experience in industry and business (Schwartz 1974).

Media and resources in education will be characterized by the extensive use of modern technologies of education, and the use of programmed individualized instruction. High-cost technologies will be employed in the form of computer-assisted-instruction and complex communication systems such as computerized resource centres. This will tend to encourage centralization in programme and resource development (Taylor 1971). Low cost technologies will emphasize audio-visual media of communication, especially in the areas of expressive and group oriented learning processes.

Educational Costs and Resources

The number of students will increase to 35% of the total population as a result of increased enrolments at all levels. This will be influenced by the extension of pre-school education and the generalization of secondary education to 18/19 on a compulsory basis, but above all by the extension of post-secondary education, particularly the growth of adult general education. Enrolment in full-time university education will exceed 40% of the age-group. Part-time adult general education is estimated at approximately two months per year for each adult, although this is an option and 100% enrolment is not predicted. The equal participation of women in full-time secondary and higher education will also contribute to increased students flows in this model (Visalberghi 1973). It is estimated that adult part-time study would approach – in terms of full-time equivalents – approximately 2½ times the number in full-time higher education (Jensen 1972).

The rapid growth of educational enrolments would offset the reduction in the number of teachers through the introduction of new educational technologies. The emphasis on small group relationships and close social interaction in education would probably lead to an improved teacher-student ratio, estimated for secondary education as 1:20. A major part of the increase in teachers might be the increase of part-time teachers especially in permanent education. It may be estimated that the percentage of full-time and part-time teachers in the economically active population will approach 5% and 30% respectively (Schwartz 1974).

In relation to buildings and equipment the introduction of new technologies will increase efficiency and reduce student wastage. There will be increased costs of new learning systems, and development costs would be high. These costs might however be offset by the increased multiple usage of educational facilities, thus reducing capital investments while increasing current cost. Increased enrolments will probably require a big expansion in capital investment. It has been estimated that capital expenditures could reach 40% of the education budget during the transition period, followed by a big rise in the current expenditure (Jensen 1972).

As a result of this rapid expansion of educational facilities the total costs of education would increase as a percentage of public expenditure and gross national product. It is estimated that 40% of total public expenditure in the year 2000 would be allocated to education on the assumptions of this model. For most countries this entails a doubling of the proportion of public resources allocated to educational services.

The means of financing education in this model are predominantly public expenditures, with a smaller role being played by private industry. This follows from the assumption that the collective importance of education would entail a strong centrally controlled public educational system. Public education will be free of charge and financed through taxation and reallocation of incomes. The collective criteria of educational policy would reduce the role of private financing to in-service vocational training, and the role of credit education on a loan basis is debatable. The social significance of education would outweigh considerations of personal gain in terms of improved income through education, and taxation of high incomes would probably contain an element relative to the costs of the education received. Adult general education might have a nominal cost to the student, symbolic of its collective importance. All students in full-time general education – young and adult – would receive a salary type of grant – *pré-salaire* (Schwartz 1974).

C. *Some Basic Problems and Tensions*

The social and educational dynamics within and between these two hierarchical alternatives suggest certain basic problems and tensions arising from their development. We restrict our discussion here to two major issues. On the one hand, the relation between economic and political objectives and the educational system, and on the other hand, the problem of educational and social selection and the potential emergence of a meritocracy.

1. *Economic and Political Objectives*

Many aspects of recent and forecasted developments of educational systems are based on assumptions about educational needs arising from evolving patterns of economic growth and employment. The tendency to base educational policy on the extrapolation of economic trends and manpower requirements necessitates a profound questioning of the exact nature of cause and effect in the relationship of economic growth and the expansion of educational systems. The essential question is whether education is an investment good necessary to produce economic growth – the development theory of education – or a consumption good which responds to economic growth and rising expectations. Both approaches are partly true, but the interactions between the two are extremely complex (Collins 1971). Nevertheless, there is a fashionable belief that the rate of economic development and the structure of the educational system are closely linked.

There are many grounds for objecting to increased provision of education on economic grounds alone. There are equally important criteria and more fundamental values involved. Beyond acquiring the necessary moral and cognitive capacities enabling him to live effectively in his society, the individual may claim the right not to be educated for a career according to the requirement of the national economy. While there is no essential conflict between the mobilization of manpower and educational opportunity for the individual in present society, we must ultimately be prepared to accept that an educational system too closely related to the productive organization of society could be an instrument of dehumanization (Halsey 1961). The economic arguments must be seen in their proper perspective, as ultimately subordinate to wider political and social criteria, and the human reasons for an extension of any given level of education may be contradictory to the economic arguments in the long run.

The stress on a high level of achievement motivation in neo-industrial society directed towards occupational success and social mobility will itself produce many problems. The inability of certain minorities to meet the achievement demands of the educational system will tend to support a severe hierarchy of formal educational success reflected in occupational status and income differentials. There is likely to be a growth of opposition, based on resentment, by those social groups failing to improve their position in society. This will include the technologically unemployable and other marginal social groups. Anomie amongst such groups will be exploited by activist and militant groups who are themselves alienated from the dominant value system. The development of the neo-industrial model will be a continuing problem of control for dominant social groups. This could dictate the emergence of new forms of repression and social control of domestic dissidence caused by stresses in the nature of the system (Harmon 1972).

The main distinction between the neo-industrial and social welfare alternatives is the transfer from the economic demand for manpower to the political demand for greater social opportunity. The logic of the mobilization of ability in neo-industrial society in practice will lead to the production of surplus talents through the educational system beyond technical requirements of occupations. Education needs to be interpreted in this context in terms of the impact of social demand and the collective needs of society. There is good reason to doubt whether decision-makers and planners will follow the same lines of development and the same options as in the past when the contradictions of neo-industrial society become increasingly apparent. However, there are few grounds for optimism as to the possibilities for social welfare society to achieve greater substantive social opportunity. The problem of reconciling economic necessities and social ideals is, and will for a long time remain, the major problem to be faced in any policy for education (Sauvy & Girard 1973). Whatever the alternative chosen, there are as many good reasons for sacrificing progress towards greater opportunity to economic and technological development, as there are for doing the opposite. The future development of the educational system may be determined by two constraints. On the one hand, education can only progress to the degree that it allows further economic growth, and on the other hand, when the main aim is to promote greater opportunity, education needs to take precedence over economic growth. With respect to the democratization of education, predictions fail to conform to reality since they lead to various sets of insoluble contradictions (Edding 1972).

2. *The Possibility of Meritocracy*

One of the main contradictions arising in both the neo-industrial and social welfare alternatives is the inevitability of meritocratic tendencies. A fully developed meritocratic system of status, cognitive knowledge as the basis of social influence, and the application of rationality to economic and social problems is to be viewed as a distinct possibility (Reuchlin 1972). Both the hierarchical alternatives are based on the continuation of a social division of labour leading to a status system dependent on the differentiation of economic and/or social skills by a selective educational system. The widespread attempt to achieve equality of opportunity through education in a class society may only lead to education rationalizing the structure of a meritocratic status system. Present trends suggest meritocratic criteria (Reuchlin 1972). The predicted consequences are that if we allow the situation to follow its natural course of development two nations could develop in each society. New forms of social selection through education could favour privileged classes and create considerable social distances between those in top level jobs and the mass of the population.

A system of "perfect meritocracy" would not only be morally intolerable but would also be doomed to failure. The only possible meritocracies are "imperfect" forms based on social privilege and scholastic advantages arising from such privilege. While imperfect meritocracy is less justifiable than a perfect form it is more possible. The errors and inadequacies incurred in not properly carrying through the democratic process in education could lead towards such a situation. The massive use of psychometry for selective purposes in rationalizing the social destiny of individuals may only have the effect of consolidating social and racial inequality (Richardson & Spears 1972). While perfect meritocracy might be a nightmare of selective permanent education, the attack on the social and scholastic advantages of the upper and middle classes would no doubt lead to an emergent authoritarian meritocracy capable of maintaining privilege. Such an imperfect meritocracy would employ combinations of hidden persuasion and selectivity to provide the quota of semi-skilled and unskilled workers needed. This imperfect meritocracy would maintain privilege and enjoy the support of the middle classes, for scholastic selection, where this is effective, favours them (Visalberghi 1973).

In both versions of hierarchical society, with differentials of power, prestige and economic rewards, education will be based on individual competitiveness, the existence of stereotype images of ability, systems for recognizing and mobilizing differentiated talents, and selective criteria of educatability.

Accordingly if the educational system continues, as at present, to be the main mechanism for the placing of individuals in different hierarchical levels of work, albeit more rationally and wisely, the system could get into a serious impasse. The major distinction between the meritocratic systems will be the greater capacity of the social welfare model to integrate less privileged groups into society (Schwartz 1974).

The broader definition of talent in this model towards common concern with social issues, as an integrative force, might help to relieve the pressure of less privileged groups from below, which is all too possible in the neo-industrial model where selection procedures would be more obvious and socially divisive. This integrative function can be viewed as a contribution to social stability if people's desires are satisfied to such an extent that there is no longer sufficient motivation for individuals to undergo the stress, fatigue and dangers of social agitation (Reuchlin 1972). The purpose of orientational guidance could be to palliate the dangers of such a social organization which can be considered as possible in the future (Reuchlin 1972). Whatever the success of the neo-industrial and social democratic alternatives in stabilizing meritocratic societies and educational systems this does not necessarily mean that the problems will be eliminated. Particularly disadvantaged minorities are likely to persist. The dominance of the economic and political requirements of a potential meritocracy gives rise to fears that education could be a nightmare of alienation and problems of social integration in a process of controlled and directed economic and social development.

PART 2: EDUCATION IN THE EGALITARIAN ALTERNATIVES

The two alternatives outlined in the first part of this chapter are to a large extent manifest in the growing movement of educational reform in most European countries. The long-term feasibility of these developments in achieving greater educational opportunity is increasingly subject to doubt. The hierarchical alternatives are highly selective of those aspects of human ability, and the measures of those abilities, which their educational systems take seriously and seek to promote. The experience of the last twenty years of educational reform suggests the very severe limits upon education as a provider of greater social and educational opportunity. There has been a gross failure to overcome the handicaps of social class in educational opportunity. When educational opportunity is seen as a means to other social ends, rather than an end in itself, the educational system seems to reflect society rather than to transform it (Bordieu & Passeron 1970). The educational system cannot be expected to compensate for a class society and the social differentiation inherent in it (Bernstein 1970). The question is whether to achieve equality for everyone it is enough to simply proclaim equality.

It is possible to consider a more positive and dynamic role for education in conjunction with other social agencies. Rather than seeing education as adaptive to the dominant social order, we may envisage a more purposive and active role for education in bringing about social change, – to see education itself as an instrument of change because of the contradictions with which it is faced. Given the problems outlined in Chapter 2, it may be that the educational system, especially in some of its spontaneous and pioneering forms, will probably have to anticipate developments in society. The more radical implications of this view for the reform of education suggest that the attainment of substantive equality in society may require more radical approaches involving fundamental changes of the criteria of educatability and achievement. A more radical policy of equality of opportunity could presuppose or entail the democratization of society and the removal of disparities in the social structure.

In examining new forms of educational provision and coordinated social policies appropriate to a more egalitarian society, major changes in the social position and influence of social groups and individuals may arise more from purposive social action than from the inherent logic of economic and technological development. The degree of equality in society has a great deal to do with ideologically oriented social action. Egalitarian educational systems are closely associated with the needs of minority and underprivileged social groups, and to a lesser degree with those radical groups currently critical of the prevailing social and educational order. These alternatives indicate that an egalitarian programme of educational change would concern action programmes of social and educational experiment to change the balance of power within education, and the relative status of socio-economic groups within society. However, there are differences to be distinguished in the orientation of egalitarian education towards either the collective interest or individual aspirations, as the two alternatives suggested here seek to elucidate.

A. *Compulsory Collective Education*

Educational Goals

Educational structures are not too radically different in this model, if the frame of reference is the social welfare model. There are, nevertheless, significant changes following upon the re-orientation of educational goals away from political stability towards communal integration. This change entails ideological commitment to the needs of the collective interest, as opposed to personal rewards for conformist behaviour and observation of the common interest. The orientation to the communal system will emphasize ideological commitment of a high level, and the promotion of high levels of engagement and involvement in communal life.

The educational system will be a strategic element of social change, and will become the key to social planning. It is through educational processes that the ideological structure will be established and maintained. The orientation to the communal system will emphasize education as the means of producing the commitments necessary to the social system. The aim is to use these commitments in the control of individual behaviour in the collective interest. These new patterns of behaviour, based on ideological commitment, will call for a significant effort to create the new "socialist" man through education. This will involve the internalization of new values emphasizing the importance of identity with the social group – individual and non-conformist patterns of behaviour will be of lower significance and actively discouraged. Traditional achievement motivations and aspirations for personal reward will be eschewed in favour of the individuals' capacity to contribute to the solution of social problems in the collective interest.

The communal orientation will stress the social group as the centre of personal identity, and will promote equality through the reduction of individual differences. Radically changed requirements in social and individual behaviour will almost certainly produce uncertainties and changes in expectations. Consequently, education will stress the problems of personal integration through group based identity, and the problems of commitment to social integration through the legitimation of new values and meanings of reality. The use of educational processes to legitimate the new ideology will stress criticism of traditional patterns of behaviour as antisocial with group sanctions leading to the rejection of old values and norms.

The collective decision-making process will be activated with an increased stress on motivation, through education, to participate in concern for collective problems. Education will develop the motivations, capacities and knowledge applicable to the patterns of collective organization in society, and in education itself. This development may be based on the understanding that the capacities of the individual are limited to different degrees. The promotion of equality will entail the development of whatever capacities the individual may possess, and will stress the maximum development of knowledge and skills in every sphere of social activity (Visalberghi 1973). Differences in capacities will be recognised in terms of their contribution to the community, and not in terms of individual gain or worth. Whatever the technical skills of the individual, he will be encouraged to express his views in the decision-making process, and the educational system must prepare for this.

Educational Structures

Educational structures in the compulsory collective society will partly resemble those of the social welfare model with major changes in educational content rather than processes. The emphasis will still be placed on public institutions of formal education and there will be no private education in any form. Education is based on the need to exclude noncollective interests from having an influence on the content of education, all forms of exploitation and individual interest being excluded. The individual would not be able to acquire education on the basis of familial advantage, nor to use education for personal gain. This follows from the important role of public education as the only agency of allocating and redistributing social and life opportunities to the individual in relation to collective rather than individual needs.

The structures of formal education will reflect the collective interest and its expression in centralized control. Pre-primary education will be generalized with an emphasis on the reduction of the advantage of privileged groups and the early development of group orientation and social skills. Primary and secondary education will be integrated into the common school, with compulsory social service for all young people, while their part-time education at this level will stress the social and political formation basic to the collective interest. Higher education will follow a period of work-experience of two or three years, and will be full-time in the traditional sense. Full-time enrolment in higher education will be open to adults on an unqualified basis according to their possession of social qualifications for advanced study. The introduction of obsolescence in educational qualifications, i.e. their restricted validity in time, will encourage re-enrolment in higher education. After the compulsory full-time school level, part-time adult education will be a feature of life-long education on a compulsory basis. This compulsory feature of continuing education will be related to political education and the concern with collective and social problems. Vocational elements of adult education will remain an important voluntary element of education at the compulsory post-school level.

The implementation of the equalization principle will mean major changes in the regional distribution of educational resources between rural and urban areas, to the advantage of the former. The redistribution of resources will follow upon integrated policies of regional development, but will entail the substantive reallocation of resources towards rural areas and deprived groups in urban areas. This will be based on the integration of economic, political and communal interest groups in the form of self-managing educational units within the overall centralized decision-making system.

Decision-making structures in education will reflect the general collective orientation of decision-making, and the individual will be involved in all group decisions affecting him directly. Participation will have more than symbolic functions, and will be basic to collective decision-making. Strong centralized agencies will be based on the extensive number of self-managing educational institutions at the regional and local level. Widespread participation in decision-making will have more affective and formative influences favouring social integration rather than critical functions. The general development of decision-making systems will entail the importance of mediating structures in which participation is encouraged at the institutional level. Such participation will relate mainly to decisions concerning the implementation of centrally-determined global policies and strategies (Federal Institute 1971a).

Collective needs and the communal orientation will dominate guidance and counselling agencies. Activities and experiences emphasizing the collective and social orientation will be encouraged and their affective dimensions will gain in significance. The social group will take on the functions of guidance and assessment to an increasing degree, with an emphasis on the individual's capacity to undergo group criticism of personal and collective behaviour. Objective criteria based on cognitive achievement will play a less significant role than social criteria. The development of group-oriented capacities, and assessment of group-oriented characteristics, will predominate in guidance systems (Jensen 1972).

Educational Processes

Patterns of curriculum development will reflect the nature of educational decision-making. Self-managing educational institutions will work within the framework laid down by central authorities. Centrally determined global goals will relate mainly to the social and communal objectives dominating the educational system and the decentralized self-management of particular institutions will mainly concern contents and learning methods (Van den Berg 1972).

The nature of the centrally determined objectives will derive from the orientation of education towards social integration. The main influence on objectives will be the need to induce the collective orientation and the solidarity appropriate to the emphasis on group needs. Learning objectives will be largely oriented towards the integration of society, and the controlled development of social change. While recognizing those objectives related to economic and technical needs, emphasis will be given to objectives relevant to the solution of social and communal problems.

These objectives will stress the inculcation and legitimation of new value systems emphasizing conformity to the equality emphasis of the collective ideology and the reduction of individualistic interests. Hence learning objectives, and the qualifications they aim to produce in individuals, will seek to integrate the individual on an ideological basis combining knowledge and values in a common orientation to reality (Jensen 1972).

The contents of the educational process will be strongly characterized by the increased importance given to socially oriented and integrative courses, which will stress the social science content in the curriculum. These general courses, with specifically ideological contents, will carry equal weight with the specialized courses relating to economic and technological needs, stressing the development of cognitive knowledge and skills especially in the sciences. At all levels of the educational system the core of the curriculum will be the basic socially-oriented aspect of education. The strictly cognitive subjects will become the basis of specialization and differentiation of vocational capacities and skills.

Practical experience, and the development of social skills in particular, will gain an important role. This practical experience could take the form of manual work within the school at the lower levels and participation in socially oriented projects at higher levels on a compulsory basis – compulsory social service. The emphasis in both the socially oriented cognitive courses and practical activities will be upon the reinforcement of the basis ideological function of general education (Federal Institute 1971b).

Some indications of the interaction strategies within the school can be gathered from the essential group orientation of educational processes. There will be a high stress on group activity and experience, particularly in the general social courses. Group educational processes will serve the purpose of interpreting the general value system in the form of collectively organized educational situations. In addition, group activities would serve the purpose of creating commitments to common goals. The flexible nature of the project-basis of the socially oriented courses would allow students to form groups concerned with identified social and political problems in their environment. In this context the teachers' role is modified to that of acting as a facilitator or animator. This basic principle will relate to all levels of education but will relate more closely to youth and adult education.

This model will tend to emphasize a close integration between educational institutions and their social environment. This will be reflected in the development of new interaction strategies between the educational institutions and the surrounding society. Since education is conceived as the key agency of controlled social change, interaction strategies within the school will give rise to increased interaction between the school and non-school environment. This interaction will not be restricted to the use of formal educational facilities by different social groups in the community, but will include new forms of collective interaction between groups of learners and learning agencies in the community (Hake 1971).

In this sense students will be concerned, in the core programmes, with the social and political problems of their own environment. They will also gain experience of the outside world by participation in various practical activities through compulsory work experience and social service. Greater participation by community groups in the management of educational institutions will also reinforce the orientation of these institutions to the outside world and the problems of the collectivity.

The role of educational technologies in the cognitive learning programmes, and consequent individualization, suggests their residual role in specialized instructional programmes as the main media dimension. In the group based *tronc commune*, with a social orientation, technologies would tend to be restricted to those permitting reciprocal communications rather than individualized media. The relative decentralization of control over contents and methods, although not over goals and objectives, would probably encourage a trend towards a diminished role for centralized learning systems. Greater emphasis would be given to those resources more relevant to the orientation to community problems and developments, and the decentralized development of learning systems.

Economic aspects

A major problem arises in assessing the micro-economic impact of this system. The traditional categories used to indicate the dimensions of educational expenditures and other economic indicators no longer apply. The limits of comparability are reached when the national accounting system is radically changed, as would be the case in this alternative. Nevertheless, some attempt has to be made to indicate the overall trends, however vague or imprecise such quantifications might be (Jensen 1972).

The introduction of compulsory permanent education radically modifies the assessment of student flows. The whole population, dependent and active, has to be considered in calculating the flow of students in a system requiring compulsory enrolment in either full-time or part-time compulsory education on a continuing basis. The introduction of compulsory adult education would lead to an explosive increase in the total flow of adult students. Such an increase in enrolments at the level of post-secondary education would require a tremendous growth in the flow of teachers. The demand for highly specialized teachers, and the emphasis on group work, would require a favourable teacher/student ratio. A rough "questimate" would suggest that full- and part-time teachers could constitute 10% and 50% of the working population respectively (part-time teaching being the equivalent of one half-day per week) (Jensen 1972).

The highly advanced concept of community usage of educational facilities on a joint-occupancy basis would reduce relatively the demands of the expanded educational system on buildings and equipment. These resources would be collectively managed by the community in relation to all learning needs and social groups, hence providing for the comprehensive provision of educational facilities. This would be a relatively labour-intensive form of education, rather than capital intensive, and indirect costs would play a significant role in the social cost benefit analysis of education. It is likely that these high costs will be tolerated as a consequence of the general social importance of education. The socialistic orientation of the society, and the assumption of an advanced level of technology, indicate the possibility that greatly improved social cost/benefit ratios would justify the educational system's claim to these resources.

The financing of education would follow upon the concept of education as a collective good, which the individual should neither acquire according to his means, nor use for personal financial gain. Consequently, the educational system will be financed on an entirely public basis, with no private sources of finance as traditionally understood. The radical changes in the distribution of income in this model would entail the free provision of education at all levels, and education would be interpreted as a general social benefit available to all. The compulsory nature of life-time education would be interpreted in terms of the redistribution of capacities to contribute to social development and the resolution of social problems, rather than the redistribution of opportunity or income in terms of individual gain.

The role of central authorities in financing education would be limited to the determination of global allocations of resources to education, the determination of priorities between different types of educational provision, and the redistribution of resources on a regional basis. Within these global targets, decentralized autonomous agencies at the regional and community level will be responsible for raising and allocating the necessary resources for educational provision. This will be achieved through community involvement in educational management, and the responsibility of community agencies for raising appropriate resources in a system of self-management. Furthermore, educational units will be, to a considerable degree, self-sustaining as a result of their practical and productive activities (Federal Institute 1971a).

B. *Voluntary Collective Education*

Educational Goals

In this egalitarian alternative, the educational system will be oriented towards individual development and self-expression through new cultural forms, rather than the integration of the individual in the collectivity through a controlling ideological system. Although education will continue to provide for the economic, political and communal dimensions of social activity, they will be subordinated to the requirements of the interests and development of the individual rather than the group. The basic orientation of the educational process will be towards non-economic and personal ends (Hake 1973).

Education will be expected to develop the individual's capacities for emotional maturity and critical intellect, and emphasize social and personal development. The personal orientation will tend to foster the innovative and creative powers of the individual, who will be recognized as the basic agency of social change through creative reflection and action. The maximization of human potential would seek the integration of intellectual and social growth through emancipatory strategies of education against all forms of domination and exploitation of the individual (Freire 1970).

To the degree that individuals share common interests and goals through social interaction and group activities, individual behaviour will be related to these social and group needs. This will lead to voluntary social participation by the individual, as opposed to the ideological legitimation of individual conformity to group requirements. In this way the individual may be stimulated by, and may contribute to, collectively oriented interaction, but will not be dominated by it. The diversity of social groups with different characteristics will require a major change in the tolerance of life-styles placing a major burden upon the education system.

This suggests very different modes of acquiring and transmitting knowledge and skills in which education becomes the central process of permanent social discussion, reflection and action (Hoernle 1970). The actual and potential capacities of learners would be engaged in determining social change through cultural creativity, rather than being channelled in predetermined socially "useful" directions. This would involve educational institutions in an open-ended relationship to society promoting the creative imagination and emphasizing the capacity of the arts and the sciences to emancipate individuals and social groups. It enables them to control their individual and common situations. Education will build upon social situations and conflicts as a basis for the creation and development of different ways of life and the social organizations necessary to support them. Education, as the key social process of a creative and dynamic society, would take on a radical perspective in the form of experimentation with new social forms (Zimmer 1971).

Educational Structures

In an educational system stressing the relevance of educational provision to individual and social group needs the distinction between formal and informal education would become irrelevant. The integration of education in the community would give rise to a situation in which formal institutions of education are deprived of their monopoly of learning (Reimer 1970). In a pluralistic educational system there would be a multiplicity of educational resources. Linking them with the learning facilities most appropriate to their needs, the educational structures of the voluntary collective society could be "deschooled" in an open, pluralistic and flexible provision of learning possibilities (Illich 1971). Informal agencies of learning, which are peripheral to the educational system in the other alternatives, move to the centre of the system and replace the formal school.

Concentration on informal learning will entail radical changes in the structure of educational provision. The formal structure of educational institutions would be replaced by community centred networks of learning agencies and media as the basis of a flexible and relevant process of education. The essence of the system becomes decentralized and deinstitutionalized through informal learning systems entailing the full use of learning resources in the community. All publicly provided educational facilities should be available to all social groups and individuals, and this should include all cultural facilities including museums, librairies, art galleries, cinemas, newspapers, radio stations, etc. (Huberman 1970). Involvement in the community would entail attachment to factories, offices and banks, social service and community development agencies, and groups would be encouraged to initiate their own informal learning through production co-operatives, social and community action groups, collective communal living experiments and creative and artistic groups (Frese 1971).

As a result of the flexibility and pluralism of the educational system, learning would be characterized by the involvement of learners of different ages meeting together in groups of different sizes, in pairs with common interests, or working alone on individual projects. This would relate also to the absence of any distinction between full-and part-time learning and the non-existence of compulsory involvement in education. All learning would be part-time in any one learning agency and there would be only voluntary learning. The emphasis on emancipatory life-long learning would reduce the significance of pre-school education, and new patterns of collective living would play a major role in reducing the differentials produced by the home background.

At the age of 15 or 16 young people would be regarded as playing a fully responsible role in social life, and would be encouraged to become involved in work experience programmes, community development and social service, and new communal forms of living. Alongside this involvement in real problems and constructive social activity, young learners would build up their specific knowledge and skills through attachment to appropriate resource and skill centres, building up a flexible and constantly changing profile of social experience, knowledge and skills (Sudale 1972). The constant interchange of productive and creative activity with specific learning programmes according to need would characterize a radically changed system of adult education in place of full-time post-secondary education and vocationally or ideologically oriented adult education. Consequently, the educational system would change from a linear structure to an "orbital network" of agencies (Hake 1973).

The functioning of a decentralized and informal educational system would have significant implications upon the nature of educational decision-making. As educational institutions merge into community learning networks, a basic requirement of decision-making will be better communication with participant groups and individuals to ascertain their learning needs. A pluralistic system would enable social groups to have their own values, goals and norms together with the right to choose between alternative educational programmes, thus changing the basic relationship between the providers and consumers of education. All those related to the educational process must be able to express their views as to the goals of alternatives provided. The role of technology and technical expertise should be reduced to that of supporting the achievement of self-determined objectives in the development of appropriate strategies.

Within particular communities and regions educational agencies would be able to establish "learning cooperatives" as the basis of an integrated and comprehensive network. Each agency would be democratically represented in decision making concerning these community and regional networks, and would be able to withdraw if they wished to do so. Any social group or individual would be able to apply for association with these networks in order to request a new agency to be established, or to set up their own agency with access to community resources.

The decentralization of decision-making logically entails changes in the methods of innovation in education. A decentralized and participant educational system in an open and pluralistic society requires a wide range of experiment in learning systems, and especially with the exploration of new links between formal and informal agencies to meet the changing learning needs of individuals and social groups. This would entail the development of distinct strategies to meet the learning needs of specific groups of students through programmes of open-ended "action research". Greater support for experiment at the margins of the system, linking formal and informal agencies, would reflect the diverse goals and values of many groups and individuals in society (Lister 1972).

The open nature of a decentralized and participant educational system would require an adequate provision of counselling services to provide guidance to individuals and social groups in making most use of the learning resources available. Counselling centres would guide learners in terms of their different needs for knowledge, skills and expressive capacities, and the structuring of different learning experiences and fitting individuals and group programmes to learning needs. Furthermore, counselling services make available the knowledge of alternative ways of learning, the potential consequences of these alternatives, and their relevance to learning needs. The role of counselling centres would be to provide feedback enabling the learner to assess the capacity of learning experiences to help him achieve his aspirations. These centres would operate independently of both resource and skill centres in a decentralized network of learning agencies (Hake 1973b).

Educational Processes

The nature of curriculum development in this alternative changes radically from that in the previous three models. Rather than goals being determined centrally by governmental agencies in terms of global targets, they would be determined by decentralized self-managing agencies. This model suggests that goals can only emerge concretely at the local level. This entails an ongoing process of goal determination in a decentralized form of curriculum development promoting greater responsiveness to learning needs. Consequently curriculum research and development would be decentralized, and the independence of development and planning groups from the financial interests of the present educational technology industry would be necessary. Development groups responsible for assembling learning materials and systems would be organized on the basis of self-managing cooperatives and be closely linked to learning agencies in the educational network. These guarantees of autonomy and independence are basic requirements of direct communication with participating groups in meeting their real learning needs (van den Berg 1972).

The objectives of educational processes promote the balanced development of the intellectual, practical, expressive, and social dimensions of the individual's capacities. Increased concentration on promoting creative capacities will emphasize divergent rather than convergent thought. This will involve the capacity of the individual to make basic choices of values and goals, to express his relationship to other individuals and towards social groups, and to develop the functional capacities necessary to control his social situation and his physical environment. This would lead to a new concept of general education as the dynamic capacity of the individual to reflect upon reality, to act upon it and to change it (Hake 1973b). This conjunction of the intellectual and the practical would stress the capacity to orientate oneself towards specific social situations, to reflect upon them, to view them critically, and to act upon them. An essential element of this orientation would be the capacity to express oneself creatively in abstract and concrete symbols as a form of self-expression and self-realization (Borghi 1973).

A further objective of the educational process would be the development of capacities of self-determination, self-reliance and self-confidence. Capacities of self-determining action will call for highly developed abilities to collaborate with others rather than to compete against them. The group basis of social cooperation requires that individuals possess the ability to work with others, to communicate with others, and to tolerate differences between individuals and groups. A low level of authoritarian characteristics will be basic to the openness of the individual to new ideas and patterns of behaviour, to innovation and creativity (Borghi 1973). To avoid tendencies towards group domination of the individual, predominant in the compulsory collective alternative, the involvement of the individual in group activity will be based on the capacity and willingness of the individual to take personal positions on issues, to understand and to act creatively (Raven 1971).

The development of educational contents and activities in an open educational system would not entail the selection of specific bodies of knowledge and information or certain key disciplines. The emphasis would be upon interdisciplinary approaches to a problem-solving basis of learning. Hypothetical thinking and instrumentalism would become significant to the identification and solution of real problems and the development of creativity. This approach would utilize the learner's needs and centres of interest in developing significant and meaningful learning experiences. Consequently, the core of the curriculum would be a series of self-chosen projects undertaken individually or with a group, and the distinction between a compulsory core and minority options would be redundant.

The different forms of enquiry, exploration and expression need to be open to all members of that society. The interdisciplinary approach would emphasize the hypothetical, exploratory, creative and interdependent nature of understanding and skills, enabling learners to see the coherence of different orientations to reality, to develop cognitive flexibility in analyzing problems, and expressing their conclusions with different symbolic systems. The forms of cognitive understanding would not lose their significance but would be assessed in terms of their capacity to produce reflexive understanding of personal and social reality. The development of new forms of integrating knowledge and values would be essential to the understanding of social reality, and the adequacy of facts and conceptual categories to the development of personal and group awareness would be required.

Technological skills would become increasingly important in enabling individuals and groups to transform their social and physical environments through action. These skills will be increasingly related to group and individual needs, and to new skill priorities required by the closer relation between humanistic personal and social development and technological capacities. A creative society will require a wider dispersal of effective technical knowledge and skills among people as citizens, producers, consumers and users of technical means. The essence of technological capacities in a wide range of social situations will lead to an emphasis on technological creativity in individuals rather than awareness of other people's creativity (Zimmer 1971).

The most significant change in this model will be the centrality of expressive activities through artistic creativity and creative social action. This would encourage the individual and social groups to relate cultural activity to every-day life through planned and spontaneous forms of expression. This suggests the possibility of creative action as criticism of prevailing views of reality and the development of alternatives resulting from new aspirations and understanding. In this sense the capacity for expression becomes a dynamic factor in personal and social development, and culture is no longer a minority product to be consumed by the majority. This would no doubt lead to a heightened emphasis on sensuous experience and exploration of the senses and the emotions. The creative arts provide the opportunity for expressing self-perceptions and perception of others through sensibility to group activity (Hake 1972).

As a result of the obsolescence of distinctions between formal and informal education in this model it is possible to discuss jointly the interaction strategies within educational institutions and with the community. These interaction strategies will stress the development of a positive programme of alternatives involving continued learning and greater educational opportunity through a decentralized education integrated with the community. Creating the opportunities for life-long learning in an egalitarian society requires the decentralization and democratization of collaborative learning in which life and society become characterized by creativity and change. The problem-solving approach central to an open education will require major changes in interaction strategies, particularly the abolition of competitiveness, the breakdown of authoritarian and hierarchical relationships between teachers and learners and the development of an open-ended relationship to society (Gras 1971). Above all the role of the teacher becomes that of a facilitator and animator working in diverse social situations where learning needs may be articulated. This flexible role gives the teacher/tutor/facilitator/animator a key role as a linkman between the various agencies in the education network. Consequently, the direct instruction aspect of the teacher's function would become a residual part of his role, and the right to "teach" would be a general social right rather than the exclusive profession of a select minority (Illich 1971).

Group work and experience should enable learners to make contact with people from different social backgrounds and situations, and with different orientations to reality. Interaction strategies must enable learners to make such contacts, to examine individual and group differences, and to experience different groups' behaviour and feeling in a variety of situations. Within these strategies learners should have a sense of importance, a feeling that they have a contribution to make, enjoy equal status and have real goals to achieve individually and collectively. Experience of diverse situations and groups should be a basis for developing capacities of individual and group tolerance of differences, understanding and co-operation (Borghi 1973).

Both group and individually chosen projects would base the organization and development of learning on the self-determination and self-management of genuine participation by learners. They would suggest the problems and questions to be investigated, and develop the basis hypotheses for empirical testing. In this way the project-based problem-solving approach ensures that pedagogic practices reflect the real social and physical problems experienced by young people and adults, children and their parents in their own community and environment. Specific stimuli may arise from current and continuing areas of interest and development at the local, national or international level. This may initiate exploratory investigation, by individuals and groups, of problems relating to the family, the school itself, workplaces, urban decay and renewal, leisure and cultural facilities, social and community development, pollution and ecology, international relations and general world problems. Above all, interaction strategies encouraging heuristic and creative thought and action would enable learners to display initiative, and undertake concrete action in their society (Tassinari 1971).

The foregoing requirements of an open-ended and emancipatory educational system integrated in its community has implications for the utilization of media in the educational process. Of greatest importance will be the decentralization of the development of learning systems to community educational networks and their constituent agencies. The need for flexible, relevant and open-ended programmes will require the decentralized development of materials and resources rather than their production by central units and/or commercial interests. Resource, skill and counselling centres, would be decentralized and developed on a community basis. A wide range of cultural agencies would be included in the media available to participants in the educational network replacing many traditional resources and means (Ontario 1973). Technological media will involve the utilization of new techniques to promote the decentralization of learning systems, and to encourage multiple channels of communication between teachers and learners, learners and learners, teachers and teachers. One-way communication and the isolation of the learner through individualized systems would be discouraged in favour of flexible and group-based communication and information systems.

Economic Aspects

The close integration of education in other social processes, the abolition of traditional educational categories, and the part-time nature of all education, make it very difficult to provide quantitative estimates of the economic implications of this model. This is illustrated in the case of student and teacher flows. On the one hand, the notions of "student" and "teacher", as opposed to other specialized roles, becomes less meaningful, and on the other hand, the traditional distinction between "students" and the economically active part of the population is likely to disappear. Consequently, estimates of the proportion of the population engaged in part-time learning and teaching will depend on the degree of intensity with which the broad conception of continuous learning in all social activities will be developed. In terms of estimating the numbers of learners involved, estimates might be made for different age ranges and the social and individual needs for them to be involved in directly educational activities. A rough estimate might be: up to 75% of time for 0 to 15 years, 50% for 15 to 20 years; above 20 years one half of the population might be involved for 50%, and the other half for 25%, this proportion varying for each individual according to need through time. The composition of the teaching body will undergo similar changes. Teaching activities would be fulfilled on a part-time basis by individuals with different competences and skills. It might be estimated that 50 to 60% of the population, including young people themselves, would be engaged part-time for up to 25% of their time at any one time (Jensen 1972).

Educational buildings and equipment would be under community control through local self-management of different learning agencies in the network. This is likely to produce significant economic gains and the reduction of capital investment costs through multiple usage of specialist facilities and the inclusion of general cultural facilities in the education network, e.g. museums and librairies, etc., as resource centres. Sharing and intensive usage of facilities would reduce duplication of provision and spread the burden of these investments. Furthermore, the reduced need for specialized institutional facilities, and the redirection of resources from high cost levels of education, e.g. university education, to low cost levels, e.g. adult education, would also reduce costs in these areas. In addition, decentralized learning systems would also tend to reduce costs through the development of new low-cost technologies.

The general trend of total educational costs could be influenced by a number of antagonistic factors. On the one hand, the decline of the professional teacher would contribute to reduced current costs, as will the above-mentioned integration of education into community life. On the other hand, the provision of free education, and the principle of positive discrimination in favour of disadvantaged groups, will raise costs. Moreover, the considerable degree of time spent in education processes of one sort or another by a large number of the population will add an additional indirect cost factor. However, it is possible that as a whole the social burden of education will be diminished relatively by the general reallocation of resources away from present high cost forms of educational provision, and the vast improvement of the social cost/benefit relationship in the longterm.

The financing of the educational system would be radically changed in this model. The emphasis would be placed upon decentralized financing by community agencies, and would require the freeing of scarce resources for new combined educational, cultural and social policies. Since all educational provision would be free, learning agencies would not raise funds from fees, and all education would be public in the sense of communal funds being the basis of their operations. Communal and regional authorities would not be responsible for the provision of education programmes, but would have the responsibility for raising the resources required by the learning agencies in the network. Any learning agency proving its viability and capacity to meet learning needs effectively would have an automatic claim on resources, and there would be maximum freedom to establish such agencies.

Economically productive units interested in vocational and specialized education and training would be required to allocate funds, according to the number of their employees, to community authorities for general educational provision and would be prevented from establishing their own programmes. This tax upon productive units would be the main source of educational finance, and would replace taxation of the individual. The individual would be guaranteed a number of "basic education years" or credits, to be used according to need through time. These would not be the monetary credits appropriate to a market and consumption model of education, i.e. Models 1 and 2, but the guarantee of free education in the learning agencies chosen by the learner as appropriate to his needs. Credits would benefit from a high "rate of interest" for each annual period of non-usage as a further illustration of the positive discrimination principle (Edding 1972).

C. *Some Basic Problems and Tensions*

Our analysis of these two alternatives lead us to consider two major problems most likely to raise tensions in each alternative and affect the dynamics of their development. These are not the only problems and tensions, but are common themes. On the one hand, there is a general problem of balancing economic and technological needs with an egalitarian educational and social system. On the other hand, there is continuing concern with the problem of reconciling an effective educational system with a participant decision-making system.

1. *Economic Development and Egalitarian Education*

A significant concern in the more egalitarian alternatives is the complex and delicate balance between the social goal of achieving greater equality and the economic and technological requirements of advanced societies. The emphasis on non-economic goals, and the subordination of the production of goods and services to collective and individual goals, is very likely to have a significant impact on the educational system and its relationship to the economic system. While the hierarchical alternatives base the selective function of the educational system on the manpower requirements of the economic system, the egalitarian models stress the need to weaken the impact of the division of labour on social stratification through the educational system. This argues the need to reduce the division of labour to what is necessary in purely functional terms, to reduce its social impact and its dominant role in the estimation of personal worth. Such a viewpoint tends to coincide with the traditional egalitarian perspective on the division of labour, and also results in a similar requirement that education should be concerned with the development of polytechnical or polyvalent capacities in the individual. It also leads to a view that in future society the democratization of education would be considered in completely new terms or would be no longer a meaningful problem (Fitzpatrick 1971).

The essential argument concerning the division of labour is not whether it is technically essential or not, but that the social results of the division of labour are only justifiable in social and political terms. Given the rejection of a hierarchical social system and the commitment to equality in social relations, the egalitarian alternatives seek social, political and educational strategies to reduce the influence of the technically required division of labour on social differentiation. Consequently, we find a stress on the role of the educational system in creating the necessary attitudes, knowledge and skills to produce the maximum possible development of skills on social grounds, rather than the minimal development of skills on purely economic and technical manpower grounds. The egalitarian aim is to produce an abundance, indeed a surplus, of skills in the population, and as a consequence the deliberate unemployment of available skills in the purely economic sector, and a more extensive development of social and political skills (Visalberghi 1973).

One particular strategy developed to reduce the social influence of the division of labour is that of the rotation of jobs. The compulsory collectivist model stresses the polarization between high and low level skills and qualifications in the economic system, and the vertical rotation of jobs is regarded as important. This gives rise to an argument that the educational system must prepare for the compulsory rotation of high and low skilled jobs. This means that highly skilled individuals will spend at least part of their time in low skilled manual tasks through a period of compulsory social service. The economic impact of this development is that the vertical rotation of jobs will not in itself considerably decrease productivity, and that economic and technological development will reduce the amount of low skilled work that is required (Visalberghi 1973).

However, a strategy of the horizontal rotation of jobs is also put forward, in which the emphasis is upon an integration of intellectual and manual work as a result of technological development and social requirements. Moreover, this perspective gives greater emphasis to the rotation of more than the purely economic functions, and does assume an extremely high level of technological development. This is more in line with the more utopian concept of social labour as opposed to the limited conception of economic or productive labour. Such a view produces a more profound influence on the educational system and a much broader conception of polyvalency resulting from the more extensive social role of the individual. Horizontal rotation thus implies the rotation of economic, political, communal and cultural functions for each individual (Hake 1971).

A further perspective offered in the voluntary collectivist society is the individual right to follow a particular economic role, whether of a high or low skill nature, that promotes his self-realization or self-fulfilment. Indeed, this stems logically from the concept of horizontal rotation of social labour in which the economic role of the individual plays a residual role in his social identity and evaluation. However, while the compulsory collective model emphasizes the role of the educational system in producing the similarity of individuals in an egalitarian society stressing the collective interest, the voluntary collective model suggests the role of education in producing individual dissimilarity in an egalitarian society stressing the individual's self-fulfilment. In the pluralistic and egalitarian voluntary collective society, both individuality and equality would work against enforced similarity and the social impact of the division of labour (Galtung 1970).

The concepts of vertical and horizontal rotation of economic and/or social functions, and the denial of the social impact of the technical division of labour, will both have important feedbacks on the economic and technological systems. Neither the compulsory nor voluntary collective models are in themselves anti-technological or against efficiency in the productive system. They subordinate the role of economic demands to social arguments for the development of the educational system. It must, therefore, be realized that in the transition to a more egalitarian social system it is possible that a serious interference with economic and technological development could occur. The question arises, therefore, as to how far the demands of the economic system should be subordinated to social and ideological demands and how far economic development can be jeopardized for non-economic purposes. Furthermore, the very achievement of egalitarian social and educational ends depends on the availability of adequate resources. The political argument thus becomes a question of the huge initial investment of resources in education required for an egalitarian programme. The long history of polytechnical education in the socialist countries of Eastern Europe illustrates how the social and cultural arguments have generally been subordinated to the economic reality of scarce resources in political decisions (Fitzpatrick 1971). However, in educational terms, it is no longer a necessity that increased expenditures on formal education are fundamental to social progress. The crushing economic burden of the continued extrapolative growth of educational systems in response to the economic and political requirements of a hierarchical society suggests this clearly (Edding 1973). In present political realities the solution is either to continue in the hope that economic growth will resolve social inequality in the long-term, or to slow down on educational expansion as a dimension of the response to the more pessimistic views of long-term economic expansion. This stable state, however, requires a massive redistribution of available resources and wealth unless social inequalities are to be preserved. The impasse in educational policy does not absolve society of the necessity to ask basic questions about the balance of material welfare and social well-being in the present and the future. The great merit of the egalitarian models is that they pose this question, and ask whether we may not have to forego certain short-term material gains for the long-term social benefit. Whether this could be achieved by collective or voluntary measures is an unanswered political question.

2. *Participation and Effective Decision-Making*

The necessary balance of collective and individual interests are interpreted rather differently in the compulsory and voluntary collective models, and are reflected very clearly in their approaches to the educational and social decision-making processes. Consequently, they have rather different implications for the formulation and realization of social and educational goals. It will be obvious that a model stressing ideological uniformity and a model stressing the pluralism of interests, both albeit in an egalitarian society, will have different views on the organization of and the degree of participation in educational decision-making at the macro- and micro-levels. To the degree that educational systems are established on the basis of an assessment of learning-needs in society, the degree of participation will vary according to general perceptions as to who is most capable of defining and determining these needs. This provides answers as to which social groups should be involved in one way or another in the decision-making process, and hence the structure of decision-making systems and the distribution of power.

The compulsory collective model tends to suggest that a strong central body is necessary in decision-making, in order to realize the socio-political ideology of a certain kind of society. At the macro-level this suggests a relatively closed system with little possibility for the representation of different groups in determining global goals or objectives, since these are to to derived from the highly crystallized ideological system. However, it is possible to expect a significant degree of local self-management and participation at the local level of specific institutions within the limits of the centrally determined goals and value system. It is difficult to see how the high degree of participation at the local level could be maintained when it is clear that real and effective decision-making occurs at a central level, and deviation from central interpretation of collective needs is not possible. Consequently, the high degree of participation at the local institutional level can be seen as either spurious, or performing a purely integrative social function that is quite divorced from its decision-making impact. The essential common orientation to collective problems and interests in the compulsory collective model would seem to require a monopoly of real decision power at the centre. This would lead to an ideological interpretation of "objective" learning needs, rather than the assessment of "real" learning needs by the participants in the educational process. It would probably lead to a situation in which participation at the institutional level would not provide a real basis for institutional autonomy or decentralization of initiative, but a legitimate basis for imposing central decision and its operation as a control mechanism. In practice, this is not radically different from the decision-making process in the hierarchical social welfare model, although participation is less in that situation, and learning needs are seen as technical rather than ideological decision.

The contrary position is required by the voluntary collectivist model. Here, we find that a high degree of participation is indicated in a decentralized system of decision-making. This entails that both decisions as to goals and means are political, thus requiring a micro-level of decision in a decentralized system with extensive institutional autonomy. The objective of this decentralization and autonomy is to promote the capacity of the educational system to respond to and meet the expressed learning needs of a diversity of social groups. The emphasis of this model is upon the pluralistic legitimacy of the educational facilities available on the understanding that these cannot be determined centrally on ideological or technical criteria. Such a pluralistic model requires that as many social groups as possible be involved in a decentralized decision-making process, and that each group should be enabled to meet its own needs through autonomous institutions. Such extensive rights of participation in decision-making, and the institutional autonomy involved, would require traumatic changes in the understanding of the roles of politicians, administrators, planners, teachers, students and parents.

The tensions between the tendencies towards centralized or decentralized decision-making systems and the consequent problems of the degree of participation by social groups and individuals raise a number of interesting implications. To what degree can education be legitimate for all social groups involved, or with interests in the input-output aspects of education, if they do not participate in the decision-making process at various levels? How far is coordination between types of educational provision influenced by institutional autonomy? Can a balanced allocation and redistribution of scarce resources take place in a decentralized decision-making process? Does a centralized system promote rigidity or innovation, and what is the chance of experiment and flexibility in a decentralized system? Again, these are important questions raised by the egalitarian alternatives in the form of a meta-theory of policy-making. However, the difficult problem remains that of basic political decision, and this depends once again on choice of social values and goals. It is, perhaps, the choice of mechanisms for determining the future nature of society that is the most significant factor in the way we shall determine the future of education. That choice, however, is the essential political question.

CHAPTER 5

SOCIAL POWER AND STRATEGIES FOR CHANGING EDUCATION

Reactions to the four alternative possibilities for the future of society and education presented in the previous chapters are relatively predictable. These reactions will be largely determined by the social position of the observer and the image of the future he projects from the conditions of that social and educational situation. Some will support one future and reject others on normative grounds. There can be no consensus as to the futures to be supported, tolerated or rejected completely. Others will deny the possibility of choice on the "objective" grounds that the future is determined by factors beyond our control as individuals. However, the need to choose a desirable future to be pursued cannot be postponed, if the appropriate strategies are to be implemented in the near future.

THE SEARCH FOR STRATEGIES

The dilemma facing education is whether it should educate for adaptation within the given structures of power in society and education, or engage in conflict with those structures and constraints. There are clearly predictable conflicts, political action and reaction, even polarization, in the transition to any one of the possible futures suggested in our report. Images of the future do not materialize by themselves but involve strategies of change. There will be supporters of certain changes, but there will also be opponents. Transition to possible futures radically different from present reality cannot be conceived of as gradual development or conflictual continuity. This poses educational issues and problems which are seldom discussed at present by those at the higher levels of decision-making in national or European education. Education for change may have more to do with education for conflict in the period of transition than accommodation to any one future. Since we cannot know the future, the importance of dialogue and participation in the choice of the future as an educational process in itself arises. The first conflict to be engaged is that of who is to participate in that process and whose interests are to prevail in the decisions taken. The view that beliefs about the future can be the source of actions in the present is in conflict with views that the future is the arena of experts. Participation in creating the future represents a form of social, political and cultural activity substantially divorced from forecasting the future. It proposes that the future of society and education rests in the hands of people – "the man in the street" – in the present and near future. Involvement in the future is a learning process in that it is a movement from present problems to some future resolution of those problems.

This perspective will equally appal the conservatives who wish to maintain present structures if not to move backward to some "golden age" of excellence, the progressive reformers who want to modify the structures to meet new pressures, and even some radicals who are blinded by their own zeal to destructure the existing structures and themselves forget the purposes of education. In proposing that the goals of education in its social context should be open to discussion and choice by all involved parties, we are not seeking to politicize education. It is already political. Education takes sides in the problems and conflicts of the present by not preparing people to deal with them. Education avoids real social and political issues, and in its decision-making and practice fails to give new vision to its own purposes or those of society in general. The danger to be avoided is to escape from the political and social aspects of the present problems in education through the technocratic illusion of concentrating on reform of structures (Drouard 1972).

It is a vain hope to look to other countries for new models of education and guides to the reform of educational structures. It is equally hopeless to concentrate on defining detailed problems such as entry procedures and follow-up between different parts of the educational structure, forms of examinations and assessments, and new contents and teaching methods. A future oriented strategy of change must first and foremost establish ways of enabling all social and political groups to share in the choice of educational goals and objectives which provide the framework for discussion of more concrete and detailed issues. It must not permit the evasion of real problems of future education, but use conflict fruitfully to produce change. In the increasing atmosphere of technocratic solutions to educational problems, there are various organized pressure groups, and as yet unorganized interests, which are and can become involved in the resistance to technocratic pressures from above and mobilize others to debate and act from below – from the grass roots.

There are no easy solutions to the need for an effective, informed and rational approach to education-changing practice. The only effective approach can be one which recognizes the various levels in which appropriate actions can be developed. The common point of departure must start with the real problems of the present, to engage in mobilizing politically conscious forces, and to develop effective and practical proposals and activity. This involvement must expose the barriers to change and confront them with new claims. There must be awareness that the radical confrontation of education in many countries by a minority does not guarantee success and does not itself explain the crisis in education. It must also be recognized that there is no revolutionary situation to be exploited immediately and also that consumer satisfaction is often used to legitimate the present structure.

There are numerous groups and institutions to be politicized and motivated to participate in future-forming activity in education. There are political parties which are in the first place interested in participating in power and controlling its exercise. It is the political parties themselves who do little to encourage participation among their own members except on election day. This produces a form of citizenship limited to consumer choice between pre-packed programmes which fails to engage people in fundamental debate about objectives. The political parties, especially the governing parties, become increasingly linked to various fashionable definitions of educational problems and solutions. Left-wing parties support abolition of early selection, the introduction of comprehensive schools, broader access to higher education and permanent education. Right-wing parties tend to stress accountability, quality of output, cost-effectiveness, and promotion of talent. These positions are reflected in the educational debate in various countries, but in most cases the latest solution to the current problem arrives just as a new problem raises its head. Just when the reforms of the 60's looked to be effective at the secondary level, the structure of post-secondary education became the problem of the 70's. The 80's will no doubt be a problem of recurrent education, although *avant-garde* elements are already proposing it as "the problem". The general result of the distance of political parties and paper radicals from educational reality is the failure to deal with basic problems at the local level.

The tendency to resolve educational problems in terms of modifying existing structures within the constraints of budgetary and financial limitations has increased the relative influence of administrators at the national level, but also increasingly at the international level. Their approach is currently concentrated on the reform of higher education or post-compulsory education in almost every European country. There is discussion of unitary, binary and comprehensive systems of provision for mass higher education, of long and short courses (OECD 1973). However, discussion of the aims of such education is absent except in the degree to which it is intended to preserve "centres of excellence" for unexplained reasons. The allocation of scarce resources is consequently carried out within the framework of assumed priorities and only marginal reallocations are envisaged, for example towards nursery education. This places innovative and experimental groups "outside the system" at a serious disadvantage, and itself produces the major constraint upon them.

An increasingly powerful group in education are those concerned in the production and marketing of new learning materials and technological media. New systems of mass education and their increasing dependence on multi-media hardware and pre-packed soft-ware are of great interest to commercial enterprises. This development opens up a potential market of consumers of vast proportions. The recent boom in educational publishing is an example of what is already developing in the educational technology industry and will gain in importance. One of the main consequences of this industry is the formation of national and international combines able to cater to the new multi-media networks in commercial terms. In the Netherlands these multinationals dominate the market and are engaged in discussion with the Ministry of Education without Parliamentary debate or control. This may lead to the market's being monopolized by the big corporations and a reduction of consumer choice. Materials are produced in terms of commercial rather than educational criteria, and the consumer is overwhelmed by products of which he has no independent assessment as to their pedagogic quality or effectiveness. Who is to control their production and distribution, who is to assess their educational desirability?

Although a very small percentage of the total education budget is spent on educational research in most countries there has been an increasing trend to use the results of educational research to support changes in educational policy. The classic case is the comprehensive secondary school reform in Sweden (Husén & Boalt 1963). Changes in educational provision based on research is obviously to be preferred to change induced by pious hopes and ideological "truths" which have been the basis of similar changes in other countries – notably the comprehensive reform in the United Kingdom. While research can provide answers to educational problems research effort is still largely guided either by the interests of the researcher or commissioned research by public authorities which obviously reflects their conception of problems. The expansion of research must avoid the illusion that researchers have a monopoly of remedies for educational problems. Researchers are in a strong position to resist the technocratic pressures to use research to justify decisions taken by those in power. This may, however, require a serious questioning among researchers of the methodological problems of choosing fields of research and appropriate techniques in experimental situations such as action research and participant observation. The danger of much present research is that it hardens reality rather than being involved in changing reality.

The trade unions within and outside education unfortunately seem to sleep out the future of education responding to initiatives taken by public authorities and employers. In general they have been successfully incorporated in the system of distributing rewards in industrial society and support reform policies in education. "Improvements" which are essential to the survival of the existing social and educational system are seen as victories for the trade unions and interpreted as the birth of a new more equal society. The early involvement of the trade unions in the provision of educational facilities for their members has diminished and been replaced by a dependence on the reformist goodwill of governments. Trade unions rarely include demands for general and occupationally relevant education in their negotiations with employers, even in the extreme case of redundancy for their members. The last thing one expects to hear from teachers unions is a discussion of the future goals of education – unless it is to justify what their members have been doing so well for years. They seem far more preoccupied with salary and pension conditions than their own retraining to meet changing needs. Their unions have also produced their own solution to the educational crisis – the reduction in the size of classes mostly as opposed to new methods.

At the local level the most important groups in education and the community are various forms of sub-cultural and citizen groups. These groups vary in their social situations and their place in the distribution of rewards. They are also distinguished by their attempts to come to terms with those situations and their relative privileges. In many cases privileged parents are active in maintaining the advantages which they can pass on to their own children, with little concern for the fact that their advantage brings about the disadvantage of others – whether financial or cultural. This is mainly manifested in the financial capacity of advantaged sub-cultures to arrange the best education for their child either privately outside the state system or by choice of residence in favourable areas with good schools. As active citizen groups these people are active locally and nationally in maintaining their advantage through various parents, organizations supporting their interests from representative school governing bodies upwards. At the best these groups maintain the capacity of conscious consumers to enforce the law in their favour. On the other hand, we find disadvantaged families often incapable of helping their children within the existing system, and unable to participate effectively in the channels of control legally open to them by law. Their emergence into active citizens groups testing the constraints upon their situation and creating new channels of control and self-determination is not rapid. Parent power in education remains a middle-class phenomena.

THE SOCIAL AND POLITICAL CONTENT OF STRATEGIES FOR CHANGE

When we propose the fundamental engagement of key social groups and institutions in the problems of present social and educational conditions, we are in fact proposing that strategies for change in education should be determined by attempts to achieve a compatibility between the advanced technological capacities of society and greater substantive social equality. We can expect the social situations of most Europeans to be influenced by the concern for finding solutions to the social, economic, political and technological problems resulting from the present commitment to continued rapid economic growth. These solutions are unlikely to come easily either from above or from the grass roots. The challenge is the capacity to develop collective actions directed at the excesses of blatent individualism while avoiding pure technocratic and meritocratic developments in society. Given the inequalities of the present, socially and educationally, this suggests social and educational policies directed towards those social groups identified as being less than equal in the present. Educational reform has less to do with social engineering to produce a meritocratic educational system and much more to do with enabling people to meet uncertain life situations. Greater equality of social and educational opportunity will remain a legitimate goal for social and educational policy in the future. There are indications that the means of achieving this are increasingly being sought in new processes rather than in changing structures.

Social and educational strategies going far beyond present policies of reducing equality through modifying the structure of education are emerging at the most exposed points in the present system of education in many countries. These experiments and innovations with new educational processes have engaged in a wide variety of problems arising from educational inequalities, and are characterized by diverse goals, methods of operation, involvement of different social groups and use of resources. Such changes often develop through the mobilization of marginal groups in education such as students and parents. Consumer dissatisfaction is an increasing source of potential innovation. Although there is no single philosophy or ideological starting point for these activities, they do suggest some common key elements in their attempts to introduce educational change which challenges the present structure of education and its supporting social groups and institutions. Since it is impossible to give an adequate and fair account of these grass-root activities, we do no more than indicate a few criteria for discrimination which may allow the reader to determine whether the activities he sees around him in his own community are characteristic of structure modifications or more fundamental changes in educational processes. It is not our intention to present a manual for would-be education changers since the process of change is ongoing and the results are not known, let alone guaranteed.

1. *The Redistribution of Power in Education*

The most fundamental consequence of the growth of innovation and experiment from below in education is the actual redistribution of influence and power over what occurs in the educational process. The emergence of new power bases in education is both the precondition and consequence of this redistribution of power. A basic assumption of many activist groups in education is that change requires the development of a responsive and open decision-making system. The corollary of this development is the encouragement of and demand for rights to participate in discussion about both the goals and means of education at all levels. The critique of closed structures of influence developed by university students in the late 1960's, in the spirit of the events of May 1968, has spread through the educational system. This has resulted in the increasing activism of secondary school students in different countries, the demand for more parental involvement in their children's education especially at the primary school level, and the claims of teachers to have a more significant role in innovation at the school and classroom level. The system of formal education has responded in a predictable way to these claims and the examples of more extensive participation provided by innovations such as the Faure reforms in France after 1968. It has accommodated to new pressure by formalizing the rights of these groups to participate in ways which do not challenge fundamentally the hierarchical distribution of power in education. The growth of indirect representation of new interest groups in established decision-making bodies does not answer the more radical claims for direct democracy at the local level. Furthermore, the claims of different groups are often in conflict. Teachers are often opposed to increased student and parental rights on the grounds that educational decisions are the prerogative of trained professionals, while in the process of pushing their own claims for greater autonomy. This has been clearly the case in parental involvement in the pre-school play group movement and teacher opposition to parental involvement in the classroom.

Despite these local difficulties the real issue of participation in decision-making centres on the degree to which centralized and decentralized systems are more capable of producing the communication, responsiveness and innovation appropriate to an open and flexible educational system. The supporters of centralization argue that goals and objectives are a concern for central agencies if vital social objectives are to be achieved efficiently. Centralized systems permit degrees of limited particpation at lower levels, usually involving professional teachers with adequate inspection. This is regarded by the supporters of participation as indicative of a closed system inadequately responsive to expressed needs. They argue for an open system of decentralized decision-making based on participation at all levels. While it is accepted that accountability to the local level can all too easily allow conservative practices to exist, middle-class local tax-payers and parents being dominant in school boards and local councils, it is argued that this can only occur in school systems isolated from the variety of interests in their social environment. Engaging in the totality of problems and interests in the community is seen as an attack on this isolation of the school from social reality.

It is difficult to be optimistic as to the short-term progress of decentralization and institutional autonomy in most European countries. Minor modifications may be expected on the part of the authorities, as during recent years in the universities, in response to the challenge from the discontent of consumer groups at the periphery. This situation is especially important with the development of a European level of decision in the near future, when most educational systems are still far from involving even the teacher in local decision-making. For the Western European countries the idea of a decentralized educational system would represent a radical challenge to their existing highly centralized and hierarchical structures which are only too likely to be reflected in any European level development. Nevertheless, there is increasing evidence that conflicts concerning objectives, priorities and effectiveness are imposing pressures leading to concessions.

The greater range of participation proposed by radical groups in practice changes the shape of decision-making bodies. The growth of wider accountability of the system to participant groups involves traumatic changes in our traditional understandings of the political roles of planners, administrators, teachers, parents and students. The mobilization of wider social forces at the local level to claim and support change in education, through the scrutiny of educational processes in themselves as problems to be solved, will increasingly impinge upon hierarchical and authoritarian systems. It involves a basic challenge to the role of the "official", "professional" and "expert" in decision-making. The grass-root critique reorders questions of desirability and feasibility, with the emphasis on possibility rather than constraints. The essential purpose of participation is not to take the heat out of the system but to raise the basic normative question, "What should happen here?" The long-term objective would be the disaggregation of policy planning structures. Given present trends in the aggregation of decision-making power in 'the development of mass education structures it would be overly optimistic to expect a progressive relaxation of their centralized and bureaucratic features. Where local initiatives have been taken by teachers and students to control their own institutions, such as the De Horst Social Work Institute and the Beverwijk Teacher Training College in Holland, or the Hornsey and Guilford Colleges of Art in England, the response of authority has been to close them or to dismiss the activist students and teachers.

2. *The World Orientation of Emancipatory Education*

To the degree that present educational structures favour advantaged social groups, a key element in new strategies is the identification of less equal groups more in need of educational provision than those normally defined as having needs in existing school systems. This leads to the idea that there should be positive discrimination in favour of these groups and their educational needs. Such discrimination is not to be interpreted as entailing merely the allocation of resources measured in per capita expenditure, or more open access to educational institutions such as entry rights for unqualified adults to higher education, although these may well be procedural consequences. For many activist groups, especially radical student groups, this entails developing action in conflict with dominant groups and their interests. Especially in adult education which is socially oriented this is interpreted as endowing less powerfull groups with capacities for self-determinining and competent action in their specific local situation. In many community education experiments the capacity of seeing the need for change is directed at developing understanding of the factors influencing their lives (Midwinter 1972).

This requires better understanding of the life situations of underprivileged groups and the fundamental analysis of the social, economic, political and cultural circumstances in society. Some life situations may be common to all social groups, such as their rights before the law in relation to employment, social security benefits, housing and local planning procedures. However, other life situations are characteristic of specific social groups and not of others, such as their capacity to enforce their legal rights, their knowledge of legislation, their capacity to commission professional support, and their links to media groups able to publicize their problems. This leads to the distinction between the life situations and educational needs of different social groups, and in this way we can understand the long-term specific and concrete situations in which people are required to develop capacities for understanding and action. Education is tested against its impact on social reality and the distribution of resources. A very valuable educational programme for people in inner city areas may be their capacity to understand and manipulate the law when their area is subject to redevelopment and they face rehousing. This is a very real situation marked by the values and cognitive interests of participant social groups. At the other extreme, the middle classes need little instruction in how to defend their interests and have the resources to do so effectively (Ashcroft & Jackson 1972).

Real problems emerge when the qualifications needed to tackle the present and future confidently are taken into account in planning educational programmes. The generalization of needs produced by thinking in purely educational terms of school subjects, or scanning the future needs of the labour market, does not allow adequately for discrimination between different needs. This is not to argue for differences in provision of education as it has traditionally been practiced in selective education. Activist groups do not argue for the generalization of provision because it is all too obvious that it will help the already advantaged and produce no equalizing outcomes for others. They argue for differences in provision in order to produce greater equality between social groups – to turn the confirming, distributory process of education into a process of redistributing educational rewards in a radical interpretation. Certain social groups seek to maintain the prevailing situation while the interests of others demands that it be changed. The capacities needed to produce change are quite different from those needed to prevent change. These capacities, and their consequences if realized, will be quite distinct and possibly in conflict. This is obvious in that their social situations will be changed in different ways. Those in advantaged positions in the present will find themselves to be less advantaged when the less than equal have been successful in making themselves more equal. If social and educational disadvantage persists in the present, this suggests the inability of certain social groups to deal with their unequal social positions. In other words, traditional education does not enable them to deal effectively with their life situations. To provide equally may be to reproduce inequality, to provide unequally may be to promote equality. This requires the qualification that unequal provision is a question of positive rather than negative discrimination (Zimmer 1971).

The fundamental engagement of the educational process in the basic problems of the social and educational system at the local level, as proposed by many critical groups, suggests the development of a reflective and conscious world orientation. By this we mean education towards critical awareness of and creativity in one's social situation and the action requirements of that situation. This form of social and political consciousness by the individual and social group is the "conscientizacco" portrayed by Freire (1972). A fundamental factor in the development of critical world orientation is the distinction between the world as defined by others and the world as defined by the individual or social group. This may give rise to awareness of the distance and potential conflict between dominant and subordinate world orientations, and the dialectic between the actual and the possible – between the reality of the present, and the potential reality of the future as defined by new aspirations and possibilities. The critical perception of social reality, however, is meaningless if it is not accompanied by the translation of understanding into goal-oriented action. It involves the capacity to change the world by action. "Learning how to learn" is no longer a cliché for adjustment to reality defined by dominant groups in society and education, but a dynamic process of "learning how to act" in the world to change reality (Hake 1972).

Critical world orientation involves the educational process in producing the capacities, the qualifications and the skills of individuals and social groups appropriate to specific social and life situations. It should equip them to reflect upon those situations, to view them critically, and to act upon them. Education becomes a powerful source of social and cultural criticism enabling the young and the old to articulate criticism and create positive responses to their concrete problems. In this way people can be enabled to look critically at what is happening around them in the world and to be actively concerned in developing solutions. A critical world orientation can become the instrument of social change and reorganization, anticipating and bringing about change in social and educational processes. The major consequence of a critical world orientation involving innovative and creative abilities could be to release energies more likely to disturb the existing social system than to preserve it.

3. *The Open and Socially Relevant Curriculum*

Many of the experiments considered here seek to challenge the a-political and a-social nature of much existing education. Educational processes encouraging a critical world orientation necessarily produce a curriculum responding to a wide range of social groups and their situations. Above all, they highlight the importance of social and political education in the effective functioning of people in a changing society and their participation in that change. The curriculum, interpreted as the activities pertinent to a critical world orientation, requires analysis of the interactions with and involvement in identifying and trying to solve real problems. This conflicts with the preoccupation of educationalists with the definition of "worthwhile activities" determined *a priori*. Learning need becomes the basis of legitimating learning activities. We find the emphasis of marginal experiments centering on the identifiable problems in the life situation of learners and their needs for action. As Tassinari (1971) points out in the case of the community activities of the *Doposcuola* in Italy, the problems arising will develop from specific stimuli in the social and physical environment. They will relate these problems to the need for new skills, knowledge and attitudes in order to arrive at solutions. In this way pedagogic practices arise from the problems experienced by young people and adults, children and their parents, in their own community. The activities of community education groups in different societies suggest that this may involve and initiate the exploration of problems relating to the family, the school itself, the workplace, urban renewal, leisure and cultural facilities, housing and social welfare provisions. It may also include consideration of pollution and ecological problems, international relations and general world problems. It is through responsible involvement with their social and physical environment that people are most likely to develop the skills to become capable of similar involvement in the future. As attempts to develop discussion of Vietnam and the Third World problem in schools have demonstrated, there is a vigorous resistance to the introduction of "taboo" subjects into the school. Attempts to introduce issues and problems such as drugs and sex, very real problems to secondary school students, are vigorously opposed by the authorities and parents in almost every country in Europe. The teacher taking initiatives is caught between the pincer movement of educational authorities from above and parent reaction from below as recent attempts to organize "Vietnam days" in Dutch secondary schools have shown. When controversial issues are introduced into the classroom by the individual teacher there is the great possibility of "unprofessional" conduct charges being pressed against him, as the Hurst affair in France during 1972 clearly shows. This is in fact an everyday threat experienced by the conscientious teacher feeling responsibility for his students' welfare. In the United Kingdom a teacher of English was suspended by his school authorities for arranging the publication of his pupils' poetry, only to be reinstated after two years of legal dispute. In the extreme case educational authorities resort to closing educational institutions where students seek involvement in controversial issues. The ultimate conspiracy against the open curriculum was the recent appeal of the French Minister of Education to parents asking them to ensure that their children were in school and not on the street confronting the police. The school itself, as a subject for debate, is the last thing to be allowed, as the ban on the "Little Red School Book" in France and the United Kingdom has shown.

There seems to be little hope that learners will be enabled by the curriculum itself to think about what they want themselves and their society to become. For the majority of young people, the appeal of the radical groups that they should be able to discuss these issues remains empty rhetoric. The possibility of learning as an authentic and creative experience leading to personal and social development is rarely supported by authority. In the United Kingdom, a controversial kit of curriculum materials on race relations produced by the Humanities Project of the Schools Council was suppressed, and a less controversial one is to be prepared. New capacities in people allowing them to display initiative directed towards changing social institutions is not always welcome. The reaction of the large multi-national Siemens to critical attitudes among its young workers was to threaten to withdraw them from attendance at the part-time school responsible for their general social and cultural development according to Dutch law. This resulted in the dismissal of the teachers concerned. Only in local community situations divorced from the economic pressure of employment is it possible for people to try out and involve themselves in experimental forms of living and acting to develop new social institutions leading to changes in social life. In spite of the example of various critical and activist groups, the transformation of social reality remains a theoretical possibility for most people.

The capacity to express oneself, "to speak one's own word", requires cognitive understanding of reality, practical skills to deal with that reality, and expressive self-realization in a changing reality. As distinguished from the existing hierarchical distribution of knowledge in society, the sum total of experiments in new educational processes argues for the different forms of understanding, instrumental skills, and expression to be opened to all individuals and social groups. While current trends in education for the underprivileged tend to stress the softer forms of knowledge, the more rigorous analysis of the social situation of these social groups demands the importance of cognitive forms of understanding – hard knowledge – in understanding social and physical reality. Technological capacities are of increasing significance to the open curriculum concerned with the generating of capacities for transforming social and physical environments. While knowledge can perform liberating purposes, in opposition to adaptation to established views of reality, instrumental skills are vital to the solution of social problems especially when technology is liberated from present interest groups. All experiences of new possibilities for living and social change suggest the need for a greater dispersion of technological skills among the population. As opposed to the individual's awareness of other people's creativity, the open curriculum requires that instrumental skills are controlled by understanding of the social need for technologies, the disciplined process of identifying problems requiring technological solutions and awareness of the resources available for technological development.

The open curriculum is further characterized by the capacity to express individual and collective aspirations in symbolic and concrete forms. The rapid growth of street theatre and creative workshops suggests a renaissance of such modes of cultural activity. This activity is based on the artistic representation of problems, aspirations and understandings of social life. The activities of such groups and the ideas of the active involvement of the individual in cultural creativity stand in opposition to the principles of social realism and the tendencies to a spectator culture. Artistic expression no longer needs to be a therapeutic phenomenon or the concern of a "gifted" minority, but can become an open concern for the majority as a heightened experience and sensibility of personal and social meaning (Silberman 1970).

There are obvious dangers in a curriculum based on the detailed investigation of the local environment. While intended to enable people to understand their social situation and cope with it, it can lead to their adapting to their social conditions rather than seeking to change them. Emphasis on tailoring relevant community education to the specific environment of the locality also works against the possibility of forming links between social groups and communities facing similar inequalities in society (Ashcroft & Jackson 1972). Social and educational strategies divorced from consideration of the social structures producing and reproducing inequalities may do little to increase people's capacity to control their own lives. Community education really seeking to affect the distribution of social influence cannot take the validity of the existing political and economic system for granted. They must provide the "hard knowledge" necessary to a critical analysis of reality and the solution of community development in a wider social context. Too many curriculum development projects directed at the less able and based on social relevance are concerned with soft subjects of low status in the total curriculum. Relevance in the curriculum can mean quietistic adaptation to, or critical awareness of reality (Hake 1973b).

4. *From Formal to Informal Structures*

The traditional logic of looking first at structures and secondly examining the activities going on within them is reversed when we see structures as institutional provisions providing the most effective situations for desired educational processes to occur. Processes give rise to their own most effective structures through experiment and innovation with alternatives rather than *a priori* prescription. In the present development of alternative provisions of learning opportunities, for example in the "school without walls", the Free School movement, and community education programmes, there is an increasing emphasis on new and often radical combinations of formal and informal learning systems to emerge from the critique of existing structures. These developments lead to a reduced role for formal structures as the core of the educational system and encourage the importance of informal learning situations in the provision of a flexible and continuing system. A major upheaval in the centre and periphery relationship is giving rise to a more pluralistic system of learning agencies, learner and teacher roles, and use of media. This has been clearly demonstrated in the Educational Priority Area programme in the United Kingdom (Halsey 1972).

Using arguments similar to those of the deschoolers, many of these innovations seek to provide the possibilities to meet learning needs at the time and place required by learners rather than to adapt learning needs to the capacity of formal structures to provide limited learning situations. The community itself is seen as an increasingly important social situation where effective learning does and can take place. In this aspect, the new initiatives differ from the progressive schools, such as A. S. Neill's Summerhill, which have little social relevance. There is a trend in community centred education towards the use of the resources and media outside the school in order to take learning to situations where it can be used in reality. The objective is to move people to act on behalf of learning rather than to isolate them from it. The decentralization of the educational system into a community based network of learning agencies encourages people to "drop-in" for learning at those agencies most appropriate to their particular needs as opposed to their "dropping-out" of present formalized structures. In the Netherlands, Germany and the United Kingdom, there has been a significant growth of education shops, workshops and advisory centres which seek to give help and guidance to parents and students concerning their learning needs and problems in the community, and to provide links between innovative groups. The point of innovation in provision is based on recognizing where learning needs are manifested and accepting out-of-school learning as a vital and meaningful component of the educational process (Bremer 1971).

Concentration on locating the social situations giving rise to both learning needs and learning opportunities is closely related to the idea of problem-centred education and self-education supported by community education experiments. This involves collaboration with constructive activist social groups which are engaged in experimentation with new solutions to the social and educational problems of the community in addition to established voluntary and official agencies involved in such development. There are also increasing demands that all cultural facilities should be freely available within an open and flexible education network intended to generate the qualifications for social effectiveness on the part of individuals and social groups. This is most clearly seen in community based experiments with cable television, video and radio such as the Open Studio in Amsterdam. In this way new technologies can be used to decentralize the information system rather than centralize it. The decentralization and participation approach to cultural activities in community education is also growing in the form of street theatre and experimental theatre groups based on community and social themes, as in the Proloog and Documentair Actueel groups in the Netherlands and the Brighton Combination in England.

Community development through greater flexibility in the educational system at the points where inequality becomes most obvious may do little to produce positive results for deprived areas. Support for marginal alternatives can be justified by the authorities as good evidence for the pluralism and flexibility of the system while doing little to change more fundamental social and educational inequalities. More often than not, official support for alternative forms of provision are seen as tidying up the ragged edges of the "good society", and does not relate remaining "pockets of underprivilege" to the social system conditioning their underprivilege. Alternatives are all too often presented independently of each other as "one-off" solutions to the "educational crisis", and each critic has his own solution to his crisis. The vague and unconvincing nature of many proposed and on-going alternatives does not captivate the groups dominant in educational decision-making. Their scepticism, of course, is supported by their control of the resources which could help the alternatives to gain greater chances of realization. It is more important, however, that the so-called crisis identified by the critics is usually based on those phenomena more symptomatic of problems than their profound causes. It is clear that the critics are virtually powerless in relation to those determining educational policies largely because of the irrelevance of their analysis to the real issues of educational change. The ideas of the critics are only too likely to be taken up and used by these powerful groups in education to the degree that they can contribute to the solution of problems facing the prevailing system. The partial analysis and solutions of the critics are impotent compared to the capacity of the education decision-takers and policy-makers to recuperate in specific situations of crisis and to incorporate those ideas which are supposed to challenge their monopoly of educational wisdom. The recently current fasion on "deschooling" among the critics of education is essentially weak at the most important level of social and political analysis. The ideas of the deschoolers are feasible only in a radically changed social and political system, yet they are not prepared to accept the consequences of that position. Consequently their ideas contribute more to the maintenance of the present system than to its change, since they are readily incorporated in the rhetoric of educational reform. The dominant system is more likely to integrate deschooling and manipulate initiatives, as is increasingly obvious in the field of post-school vocational and technical training by industry. Educational authorities are wide awake to challenging ideas, as the international "magnificent seven" led by Edgar Faure have illustrated with the incorporation of deschooling in their recent UNESCO report (UNESCO 1972).

TOWARDS MORE EFFECTIVE INNOVATION IN EDUCATION

A dynamic policy of education for the present and future is more than a new educational policy, because it is supposed to affect the whole social, political and economic order of society. This means a move beyond modifications of existing structures and sophisticated intervention strategies within those structures. It needs to tackle more fundamental dimensions of gross social and economic inequalities in present society through integrated social and educational strategies. Such a comprehensive social and educational policy, when guided by the analysis of the needs of specific social groups, could produce real and substantive changes in the distribution of life chances. Discrimination in favour of less powerful groups could lead to a constructive programme for the redistribution of resources and rewards between individuals, families, communities and institutions. This is not only an argument for more money and resources to remove inequality, but an awareness that some sectors of the educational system have too many resources in relation to the needs of others. In addition, the educational system itself may receive too great an allocation of resources compared to other social and community services also instrumental in seeking to remove inequalities. Discrimination in a purposeful and positive sense entails a total strategy at every level of education, intra-school between pupils, inter-school between rich and poor neighbourhoods, within the system and outside it through social policy. Available resources fall far short of the demands of the formal school system if it is to be indefinitely extended as at present. However, the effectiveness of achieving greater equality through education is open to increasing doubt, and the cost-effectiveness of education in attaining its stated social purposes is suspect. There are no simple answers to these problems of the most effective strategies to be pursued. We need to know much more about the effectiveness of alternatives. The one single change in priorities required as a consequence of this is the devotion of a much greater percentage of the education budget to research and evaluation of the formal school and potential new forms of provision.

The major issue here is the need for a more effective strategy of experiment and innovation in education to evaluate the best ways of meeting the learning needs of different social groups. There is a basic need for a broadly based system of social and educational research questioning the capacity of existing systems to promote effective innovation at the periphery. If the aim is to find out "what works" and to know why, it will be necessary to develop strategies with a maximum definition of the needs to be met. This calls for better consultation and communication with participant groups concerning their needs. This is a question of giving support to experiment at the periphery and a reduction in central initiatives. Greater communication between the providers and consumers of education requires the involvement of interest groups in a variety of community and educational conditions. The outcome might be a significant increase in soundly based social and educational action research programmes which explore the potentials of new forms of provision. When this is based on particular needs of specific local areas the community can itself be involved in planning its own future. Social action research could be the catalytic agent focusing attention on the social basis of the inequalities experienced in these areas educationally and support the rigorous search for new solutions.

However, it needs to be pointed out that much so-called action research in community based education is surrounded by a mystique that prevents its practitioners from questioning their own action and its relationship to the needs of those they claim to help. They often fail to examine questions about the composition of the community, different perceptions of community and different interests in the community. There tends to be a strong element of populism and romanticism in the "make the people happy" approach to community development. There is a significant tendency towards middle-class pioneers investing great efforts in building up communities, becoming anxious to retain control over the artificial activities they create, and becoming disillusioned when the "community" collapses as soon as they withdraw. Community schools are more often attempts to build artificial communities rather than the attempts of real communities to establish and develop their educational potentials (Ball & Ball 1973).

Action research must be firmly based on sound theory and evaluation, rather than the justification of what actually happens because somebody happens to also believe in it. Unfortunately, all too many experimental groups are resistant to outside evaluation of their activities, and the lack of evaluation may contribute to the extremely short life of many alternatives. To this end, the existing national and educational agencies in the field of educational policy, such as UNESCO and CERI, could put more of their resources at the disposal of experiments and innovations at the periphery. At the moment, their efforts are too often determined by the effort to support the existing system and its survival capacity as opposed to an evaluation of it. This support to unofficial change strategies could be especially important in the provision of technical advice, evaluation of programmes, and comparative study of programmes between countries. They could also do more to facilitate the exchange of information between experimental groups and the development of new advisory services in the field. The existing international clearing houses tend to concentrate on official reform measures to the detriment of valuable experiences elsewhere. There is a gradual development of such information systems on alternatives in certain countries, but their resources are limited. There is a serious need at the present time of questioning and experimenting in education to establish an international clearing-house for the exchange of information and ideas on alternatives in educational provision which would enable the local level of experiment in the different countries to learn from each other.

The decision to allocate greater resources to experiment and innovation depends on more basic political issues in society. This is a question of determining what proportion of resources should go to supporting on-going systems and present commitments, and how much should go to strategies of change at the local level. The many on-going experiments and innovations in education at the local community school level are of great significance. They point out the shortcomings of the present system at the level where it is experienced, and they also have experience of the effectiveness of different ways of operating to produce change vis-à-vis the established system and groups resistant to change. However, the embryonic forms of alternatives are only secure to the degree that they do not challenge the existing centres of political and social influence in education. Innovations based on technological media are safe since they do not challenge the centralized control over the information to be carried. School-based extensions of the educational system do not challenge the system because they are largely based on integrationist and manipulative pressures. Innovations caught between the traditional boundary structures of social and educational policy, such as adult education and the youth services, are in danger of being used as safety-valves. They can be manipulated through the recuperative powers of the system. Open-ended action research dealing with the social and educational needs of the less equal may well challenge the system and is very vulnerable to counter measures by dominant social and educational interest groups.

If a solution to the "education crisis" is to be found, it may be first necessary to recognize that it is in fact a social crisis arising from severe inequalities in modern society. We may find it necessary to support alternatives already in existence, to initiate strategies encouraging new experiments if the connection is to be made between learning to know and to act. To enable the individual to understand reality for himself and to act to change that reality constitutes a radical challenge to the present distribution of knowledge and power in society. The economic and political structures of the Western and Eastern European countries could not withstand the impact of giving more people access to knowledge and opportunities to act in the service of their own interests.

BIBLIOGRAPHY

ALBERTA (1972) *A Choice of Futures*, report of the Alberta Commission on Educational Planning, Government Printing House, Edmonton, Alberta.

ANDERSSON, B. E. (1970) *Studies in Adolescent Behaviour*, Almqvist & Wiksell, Stockholm.

ASHCROFT, B. & K. JACKSON (1972) *Adult Education, Deprivation and Community Development – A Critique*, University of Liverpool.

BALL, M. & C. BALL (1973) *Education for Change: Community Action and the School*, Penguin, London.

BARAN, P. (1970) *Political Economy of Growth*, M. R. Press, New York.

BAUDALET & ESTABLET (1971) *L'école capitaliste en France*, Maspero, Paris.

BELL, D. (1967) Notes on the Post-Industrial Society, in *Public Interest*, New York.

BENGTSSON, J. (1971) *The U.68 Committee and Secondary Education in Sweden*, mimeo, ECF, Amsterdam.

BENN, C. & B. SIMON (1972) *Half-Way There*, 2nd Edition, Penguin, London.

BERG, I. (1970) *Education and Jobs: The Great Training Robbery*, Praeger, N.Y.

VAN DEN BERG, A. & L. POSTMA (1970) *Development of a Model for Curriculum Research and Development*, mimeo, Ledo Project, University of Groningen.

VAN DEN BERG, A. (1972) *Alternative Models for Curriculum Development*, mimeo, ECF, Amsterdam.

BERNSTEIN, B. (1970) A Critique of the Concept of Compensatory Education, in *Education for Democracy*, Eds. D. Rubenstein & C. Stoneman, Penguin, London.

BILDUNGSRAT (1970) *Empfehlungen der Bildungskommission*, Stuttgart.

BIRNBAUM, N. (1970) *The Crisis of Modern Industrial Society*, Oxford University Press, London.

BORDIEU, P. & DEBORD (1967) *La société du spectacle*, Editions du Champ Libre, Paris.

BORDIEU, P. & J. C. PASSERON (1967) *Les héritiers*, Editions de Minuit, Paris.

BORDIEU, P. & J. C. PASSERON (1970) *La reproduction*, Editions de Minuit, Paris.

BORELLI, M. (1972) *The School and Capitalist Development*, Mimeo, Nuffield Teachers Project, University of York.

BORGHI, L. *et al.* (1974) *Perspectives in Primary Education*, Nijhoff, The Hague.

CALDER, N. (1969) *Technopolis*, MacGibbon & Kee, London.

CICOUREL, A. V. & J. KITUSE (1963) *The Educational Decision-makers*, Bobbs-Merrill, Boston.

COLLINS, M. (1971) *Functional and Conflict Theories of Educational Stratification*, American Sociological Review, vol. 36.

COOMBS, P. (1968) *The World Crisis in Education*, Oxford University Press, New York.

COUNCIL OF EUROPE (1971) *Permanent Education*, Strasbourg.

CROSLAND, A. (1956) *The Future of Socialism*, Routledge, London.

CROSLAND, A. (1970) *A Social Democratic Britain*, Fabian Society, London.

DEBRAY, R. (1967) *Revolution within the Revolution*, M. R. Press, New York.

DOUGLAS, J. W. B. (1969) *All our Future*, Davis, London.

DROUARD, A. (1972) Education, in *Europe Tomorrow*, Ed. R. Mayne, Collins, London.

THE ECOLOGIST (1972) *Blueprint for Survival*, Penguin, London.

EDDING, F. (1973) *Higher Education in a Future System of Universal Recurrent Education*, Info-FEC, ECF, Amsterdam.

EHRLICH, P. (1970) *Population, Resources and Environment*, W. H. Allen, London.

FAITH, S. & A. J. JANSEN (1973) An Interim Report on a Cross National Project on Alternative Futures for Agriculture, *Futures*, September, London.

FEDERAL INSTITUTE (1971a) *The Development of Polyvalent Education in Yugoslavia*, mimeo, ECF, Amsterdam.

FEDERAL INSTITUTE (1971b) *The Social Objectives of Self-Management in Yugoslav Secondary Education*, mimeo, ECF, Amsterdam.

FERKISS, V. (1969) *Technological Man*, Mentor Books, New York.

FITZPATRICK, S. (1971) *The Ministry of the Enlightenment*, Cambridge University Press, London.

FOLGAR, J. K. & C. B. NAM (1965) *Trends in Education in Relation to the Occupational Structures*, Soc. of Education, Vol. 38, No. 1.

FORD, J. (1970) *Social Class and the Comprehensive School*, Routledge & Kegan Paul, London.

FORD, G. W. & L. PUGNO (Eds.) (1964) *The Structure of Knowledge and the Curriculum*, Rand McNally, New York.

FOUCAULT, M. (1961) *The Great Lock-up*, Random House, New York.

FOURASTIÉ, J. (1965) *Les 40.000 heures*, Laffont-Gonthier, Paris.

FRANK, A. (1967) *Capitalism and Underdevelopment in Latin America*, Penguin, London.

FREIRE, P. (1970) *Pedagogy of the Oppressed*, Herder & Herder, New York.

FREIRE, P. (1972) *Cultural Action for Freedom*, Penguin, London.

FRESE, H. H. (1971) in *Permanent Education*, Council of Europe, Strasbourg.

FRESE, H. H. (1972) Permanent Education – Dream or Nightmare? in *Education and Culture*, Council of Europe, Strasbourg.

GABOR, D. (1972) *The Responsible Society*, Faber, London.

GAGNÉ, R. (1965) *The Conditions of Learning*, Holt, Rinehart & Winston, New York.

GALBRAITH, J. K. (1967) *The New Industrial Estate*, Hamish Hamilton, London.

GALTUNG, J. (1970a) Pluralism and the Human Future, in *Futures*, No. 3, London.

GALTUNG, J. (1970b) *Images of the World in the Year 2000*, mimeo.

GOLDTHORPE, J. *et al.* (1968) *The Affluent Worker*, 3 vol., Cambridge University Press, London.

GOODLAD, J. (1967) *The Changing School Curriculum*, Fund for Advancement of Education, New York.

GRAMSCI, A. (1959) *The Modern Prince*, International Publishers, New York.

GRAS, A. (1971) *The Progressive Critique of Educational Ideologies in France since May 1968*, mimeo, ECF, Amsterdam.

GROSS, B. (1966) *A Great Society?*, Random House, New York.

HABERMAS, J. (1970) *Towards the Rational Society*, Heinemann, London.

HAKE, B. J. (1971) *Education in China*, mimeo, ECF, Amsterdam.

HAKE, B. J. (1972) Social and Cultural Future for Western Europe, in *Possible Futures of European Education*, Nijhoff, The Hague.

HAKE, B. J. (1973) Values, Technology and Futurology, in *Analysen und Prognosen*, January, Berlin.

HAKE, B. J. (1975) *Education for Emancipation*, Nijhoff, The Hague.

HALL, P. (1972) *Alternative Social Futures in Plan Europe 2000*, mimeo, ECF, Amsterdam.

HALSEY, A. H. (1961) *Ability and Educational Opportunity*, OECD, Paris.

HALSEY, A. H. (1972) *Education Priority Areas*, HMSO, London.

HAMPDEN-TURNER (1971) *Radical Man*, Macmillan, London.

HARBISON F. H. & C. MYERS (1964) *Education, Manpower and Economic Growth*, McGraw Hill, New York.

HARMAN, W. (1972) *Changing United States Society: Implications for Schools*, in *Alternative Educational Futures in the United States and in Europe*, OECD, Paris.

HAYTER, T. (1971) *Aid as Imperialism*, Penguin, London.

HELMER, O. (1966) *Social Technology*, Macmillan, New York.

HINDESS, B. (1971) *The Decline of Working Class Politics*, Merlin Books.

HOERNLE, E. (1970) *Grundfragen Proletarischer Erziehung*, von Werder & Wolf, Frankfurt.

HOLLEY, D. (1971) *Schools, Society and Humanity*, MacGibbon & Kee, London.

HUBERMAN, M. (1970) *Reflections on the Democratization of Secondary and Higher Education*, mimeo, UNESCO, Paris.

HUSÉN, T. (1972) The Purposes of Futurologic Studies in Education, in *Alternative Educational Futures in the United States and in Europe*, OECD, Paris.

HUSÉN, T. & G. BOALT (1967) *Educational Research and Educational Change*, Almqvist & Wiksell, Stockholm.

INTERNATIONAL BUREAU OF EDUCATION (1970) *Educational Trends in 1970*, Geneva.

ILLICH, I. (1971) *Deschooling Society*, Harper Row, New York.

JALÉE, R. (1968) *The Third World in the World Economy*, M. R. Press, New York.

JANNE, H. (1970) *Le temps du changement*, Gérard, Verviers.

JANNE, H. (1972) Future Policy for Education, in *Education and Culture*, Council of Europe, Strasbourg.

JANNE, H. & J. GÉMINARD (1973) *The Educational Needs of the 16-19 Age Group*, Council of Europe, Strasbourg.

JANTSCH, E. (1967) *Technological Forecasting in Perspective*, OECD, Paris.

JENCKS, C. (1973) *Inequality: A Reassessment of Family and Schooling in America*, Allen Lane, London.

JENSEN, S. (1972) Numerical and Systems Forecasts, in *Possible Futures of European Education*, Nijhoff, The Hague.

KAHN, H. & A. WIENER (1967) *The Year 2000*, Macmillan, New York.
KAHN, H. & S. BRIGGS (1972) *Things to Come*, Macmillan, New York.
KAHN, H. (1972) Inventing the Future in spite of Futurology, in *Futures*, London.
KEDDIE, N. (1971) Classroom Knowledge, in *Knowledge and Control*, M. Young (Ed.), Collier-MacMillan, London.
KOLAKOWSKY (1971) *Marxism and Beyond*, MacGibbon & Kee, London.
KORNHAUSER, W. (1960) *The Politics of Mass Society*, Free Press, New York.
KYÖSTIÖ, H. (1972) *The Role of Schooling in Society*, mimeo, University of Helsinki.
KUHN, T. (1962) *The Structure of Scientific Revolutions*, Chicago University Press.

LAING, R. (1967) *The Politics of Experience*, Penguin London.
LEONARD, G. (1971) *Education and Ecstacy*, Dell, New York.
LEFEVBRE, H. (1967) *Contre les Technocrates*, Ed. Minuit, Paris.
LIPSET, S. M. (1964) *The First New Nation*, Doubleday, New York.
LISTER, I. (1972) The Concept of Deschooling – An English Viewpoint, in *Education and Culture*, Council of Europe, Strasbourg.

MACCLELAND (1967) *The Achieving Society*, Appleton-Crofts, New York.
MANDEL, E. (1970) *Marxist Economic Theory, The Economy of the Transition*, Merlin Books.
MARCUSE, H. (1969) *An Essay on Liberation*, Beacon Press, New York.
MARSDEN, D. (1970) How Comprehensives Missed the Tide, in *Education for Democracy*, Eds. D. Rubenstein & C. Stoneman, Penguin, London.
MASON, M. (1970) *Patterns of Dominance*, Oxford University Press, London.
MEADOWS, D. *et al.* (1972) *The Limits to Growth*, Universe Books, New York.
MIDWINTER, E. (1972) *Priority Education*, Penguin, London.
MISHAN, E. (1972) *Thinking of the Future*, in Fears and Hopes for European Urbanization, Nijhoff, The Hague.
MORIN, E. (1969) *Mai 1968: La Brèche*, Ed. Minuit, Paris.
MORIN, E. (1970) *Journal de Californie*, Ed. Minuit, Paris.
MYRDAL, G. (1968) *Asian Drama*, Oxford Univ. Press. London.

NAVILLE, P. (1963) *Vers l'automation sociale*, Maspero, Paris.
NEVILLE, R. (1970) *Play Power*, Paladin, London.

OECD (1971) *Educational Policies for the 1970's*, Paris.
OECD (1971a) *New Approaches in Secondary Education*, Paris.
OECD (1971b) *Equal Educational Opportunity*, Paris.
OECD (1971c) *Recurrent Education*, Paris.
OECD (1971d) *Curriculum towards the 80's*, Paris.
OECD (1972) *Strategies of Compensation*, Paris.
OECD (1973) *Short-Cycle Higher Education*, Paris.
OETTINGER, I. (1968) *Run, Computer, Run*, Harvard University Press.
ONTARIO (1973) *The Learning Society*, a report of the Commission on Post-Secondary Education in Ontario, Government Printer, Ottawa.

PARKIN, F. (1971) *Class Inequality and Political Order*, MacGibbon & Kee, London.

PASSERON, J. P. (1967) *Education, développement et démocratie*, Mouton, The Hague.

PETERSON, A. (1967) *The Future of Education*, Faber & Faber, London.

PLATT, J. (1970) How Men Can Plan Their Future, in *Futures*, London.

POIGNANT, R. (1973) *Education in the Industrialised Countries*, Nijhoff, The Hague.

RAVEN, J. (1971) Education in the Last Quarter of the 20th Century, in *Educational Sciences*, Budapest.

RÉE, H. (1970) School in the 1980's, in *Dear Lord James*, Ed. T. Burgess, Penguin, London.

REICH, C. (1968) *The Greening of America*, Random House, New York.

REIMER, E. (1970) *School is Dead*, Penguin, London.

REUCHLIN, M. (1972) *Individual Orientation in Education*, Nijhoff, The Hague.

RICHARDSON, *et al.* (1972) *Race, Culture and Intelligence*, Penguin, London.

RICHMOND, K. (1971) *The Educational Revolution*, Methuen, London.

RICHTA, R. (1968) *La Civilisation au Carrefour*, Anthropos, Paris.

ROSZACK, T. (1969) *The Making of a Counter-Culture*, Doubleday, New York.

SAUVY, A. (1973) *La Croissance Zéro*.

SAUVY, A. (1973) *Access to Education*, Nijhoff, The Hague.

SCHWARTZ, B. (1974) *Permanent Education*, Nijhoff, The Hague.

SHAPLIN, N. & H. OLDS (1964) *Team-Teaching*, Harper Row, New York.

SILBERMAN, C. (1970) *Crisis in the Classroom*, Random House, New York.

SIMPSON, A. (1972) *Adult Education in Europe Today and Tomorrow*, Council of Europe, Strasbourg.

SKINNER, B. (1968) *Technology of Teaching*, Appleton Century, New York.

VAN STEENBERGEN, B. (1970) *Critical and Establishment Futurology*, mimeo.

SUDALE, T. (1971) *Continuing Education*, Council of Europe, Strasbourg.

SUPPES, P. (1971) in *Alternatives in Education*, Ed. B. Rusk, University of London Press, London.

TASSINARI, G. (1971) *The Significance of the Doposcuola and Quartiere Movement*, mimeo, ECF, Amsterdam.

TAYLOR, R. (1971) *Resources for Learning*, Penguin, London.

TITMUS, R. (1962) *Income Distribution and Social Change*, Routledge, London.

TOFFLER, A. (1971) *Future Shock*, Random House, New York.

TOURAINE, A. (1968) *Le mouvement de mai ou le communisme utopique*, Ed. Minuit, Paris.

TOURAINE, A. (1970) *La société post-industrielle*, Ed. Minuit, Paris.

UNESCO (1972) *Learning to Be*, Harrap, London.

VAIZEY, J. (1967) in *Social Objectives and Educational Planning*, OECD, Paris.

VERMOT-GAUCHY, M. (1965) *L'éducation pour demain*, Editions du Rocher, Monaco.

VISALBERGHI, A. (1973) *Education and Division of Labour*, Nijhoff, The Hague.

WERTHEIM, W. (1973) *Evolution and Revolution*, Penguin, London.
WILLENER, A. (1970) *The Action Image of Society*, Tavistock, London.

YOUNG, M. (Ed.) (1971) *Knowledge and Control*, Collier-MacMillan, London.

ZIEGLER, W. (1972) An Approach to the Futures-Perspective in American Education, in *Alternative Educational Futures in the United States and Europe*, OECD, Paris.
ZIMMER, J. (1971) *Aspects of a Curriculum for Working Class Children*, mimeo, ECF, Amsterdam.

BIOGRAPHICAL NOTES

JARL BENGTSSON has undertaken educational research at the University of Göteborg, and is currently working on the recurrent education programme of the Centre for Educational Research and Innovation, OECD in Paris.

ALBERT VAN DEN BERG was a history teacher before taking up curriculum research at the University of Groningen, and is presently Director of Research and Development at the Kohnstamn Institute for Educational Research, Amsterdam.

DIETER BERSTECHER did research work in the economics of education at the Max Planck Institut für Bildungsforschung in West Berlin, and is now a consultant for UNESCO in South East Asia.

ALAIN GRAS is a sociologist, and worked at the University of Lund before taking his present position at the Ecole des Hautes Etudes in Paris.

BARRY HAKE was a teacher and later lecturer in the sociology of education, and was engaged in futures research with Plan Europe 2000 from 1970 to 1973.

IGNACE HECQUET worked as a research economist with OECD before moving to the Department of Research and Development at the University of Louvain.

IAN LISTER taught history before working for the British Council in Austria, and is a lecturer in education at the University of York.

GASTONE TASSINARI has been a teacher and is now a lecturer in social education at the Institute of Education at the University of Florence.

JÜRGEN ZIMMER taught before working on curriculum research at the Max Planck Institute in Berlin and is now doing research on pre-school education at the Deutsches Jugend Institut in Munich.

INDEX

PREVIOUSLY PUBLISHED IN PLAN EUROPE 2000. PROJECT EDUCATION

1. Possible Futures of European Education, by Stefan Jensen. 1972. XVIII, 270 p. Guilders 32.50

2. Individual Orientation in Education, by Maurice Reuchlin. 1972. XI, 76 p. Guilders 13.50

3. Access to Education, by Alfred Sauvy. 1973. V, 157 p. Guilders 22.50

4. Education and Division of Labour, by Aldo Visalberghi. 1973. 189 p. Guilders 27.50

5. Education in the Industrialised Countries, by Raymond Poignant. 1973. XII, 324 p. Guilders 52.50

6. A University of the Future, by Gaston Deurinck a.o. 1974. XI, 195 p. Guilders 30.–

7. Perspectives in Primary Education, bij Lamberto Borghi a.o. 1974. VIII, 250 p. Guilders 38.50

8. Permanent Education, by Bertrand Schwartz. 1974. XXIII, 246 p. Guilders 37.50

9. Talent, Equality and Meritocracy, by Torsten Husén. 1974. IX, 157 p. Guilders 32.50

GPSR Compliance

The European Union's (EU) General Product Safety Regulation (GPSR) is a set of rules that requires consumer products to be safe and our obligations to ensure this.

If you have any concerns about our products, you can contact us on ProductSafety@springernature.com

In case Publisher is established outside the EU, the EU authorized representative is:

Springer Nature Customer Service Center GmbH
Europaplatz 3
69115 Heidelberg, Germany

Batch number: 10830943

Printed by Printforce, the Netherlands